WILDERNESS
ETHICS

WILDERNESS ETHICS

Preserving the Spirit of Wildness

Foreword by Roderick Frazier Nash

Laura and Guy Waterman

THE COUNTRYMAN PRESS
Woodstock, Vermont

Published by The Countryman Press
P.O. Box 748, Woodstock, Vermont 05091
Distributed by W.W. Norton & Company, Inc., 500 Fifth Avenue, New York, NY 10110

Cover design by Bodenweber Design
Cover photograph by Sara Gray from oi2.com
Text design by Karen Savary
Interior art by Beth Krommes

Printed in the United States of America
Printed on Recycled Paper

**Library of Congress
Cataloging-in-Publication Data**
Waterman, Laura.
Wilderness ethics: preserving the spirit of wildness/Laura and Guy Waterman;
foreword by Roderick Frazier Nash.
p.   cm.
Includes index.
ISBN 0-88150-256-1
1. Wilderness areas—United States
2. Wilderness areas—United States —Recreational use.
3. Nature conservation—United States—Moral and ethical aspects.
4. Nature conservation—United States—philosophy.
5. Wildlife conservation—Moral and ethical aspects.
6. Wildlife conservation—United States—philosophy
I. Waterman, Guy.
II. Title
QH76.W38   1993
333.78'2—dc20

Extracts from the following sources have been reprinted with kind permission: Tony Goodwin, "Rangers in the Night," *Adirondack Life*, January–February 1990; James North, "Preserving the Wilderness Idea," *American Hiker*, Spring 1990; Steve Page, "Speck Pond: Analysis of a Backcountry Shelter," *Appalachia Bulletin*, December 1972; Mike Usen, "Mountain Biking Comes East," *Appalachia Bulletin*, May 1990; Robert Proudman, "Accidents: Search and Rescue of David Cornue and Jane Gilotti," *Appalachia*, December 1975; Robert Kruszyna, letter-to-the-editor, *Appalachia*, December 1975; Peter M. Leschak, "Facing the Elephant," *Backpacker*, April 1990; Lisa C. Kernek, "Massive Search Turns Up Man Who Says He Wasn't Lost," *The Berkshire Eagle*, May 2, 1991; letter from Peter Crane to the authors; letter from Sandy Eldridge to the authors; Don Jordan, "To Our Nation's Fisheries," *Izaak Walton League of America, Outdoors Ethics Newsletter*, Spring 1991; letter from Allen Koop to L&GW; paper by Robert Kruszyna, "The Case Against Search and Rescue"; letter from James P. McCarthy to the authors; Alan Smith, "The Mount Washington Map Project, Part III," *Mount Washington Observatory News Bulletin*, Fall 1988; Hugh Neil Zimmerman, "From the President's Desk," *Trail Walker*, October–November 1990; letter from Nathaniel Scrimshaw to the authors.

10 9 8 7 6 5 4

*Dedicated
to a score of our friends 10 years old or younger—
Miah and Amanda
James and Scott
Clara and Ben
Emma Rose
Christine and Danny
Anna and Jay
Uli
Justin
Arran and Aslyn
Morgan, Rob, and Liza
Mary Kalisi
and of course Jessie*

*with the fervent hope that 10 or 20
or 50 years from now, they will still
find wildness and adventure and mystery
and wonder in the mountains.*

Also by Laura and Guy Waterman

Contents

Guy Waterman: An Appreciation

SINCE GUY, MY HUSBAND, WALKED out our door and up the mountain on February 6, 2000, not planning to come back down again, I have received a staggering flood of mail. At times it felt overwhelming as I attempted to work my way to the surface of the pile, only to be submerged again when I visited my mailbox at our village post office.

Friends assured me I really didn't need to answer all these letters: that a reply was not required of those in a bereaved state. But, I told them, all these people are reaching out to me; I want to reach back. Indeed, answering these letters—engaging in a bit of dialogue with so many people—was more healing than I could have ever known. I was sole witness to the outpouring of love and concern and admiration for Guy that perhaps no one can experience while alive. Even for those who are left, few experience such an outwash of expression.

I heard from people I had never met, and who knew Guy only through our books. I heard from people who had met Guy up on the Franconia Ridge, working on the trail we had maintained since 1980. Often hikers stopped to talk with us about the alpine vegetation and our stewardship work. Some paused to help us move a rock or two in an effort to better define the footpath. I heard from one who had never met Guy up there, but had walked the ridge,

knew of our connection with it, and loved it, as we did. I heard
from people who had climbed rock with Guy, and who wrote how
Guy had instilled in them a lifelong love of climbing.

I doubt Guy could have believed how he was loved, how he
had changed others' lives, how so many relished his stories and
humor, how his eloquence and loyalty to preserving the wildness of
our mountains *did* touch others. I doubt he would have believed,
even, how much just plain fun he was to be with, either here at our
homestead or in the mountains. "Pixieish" was a word frequently
repeated in those letters. Also "dedication," "conviction," "influential," "idealist," "a symbol," "a sense of mission." One friend wrote,
"I kept thinking of Guy on those great hikes and the 'Guy Spirit'...
sharing his stories of the mountains and special places like Scott's
Cascades. Guy's spirit will be with us in all those special places in
our forest."

Guy was particularly disappointed that our book *Wilderness
Ethics* didn't have more impact. Although he felt many of the key
people in mountain management read it and heeded its message—
"fit audience find, though few," to quote his beloved poet John
Milton—it was not enough.

Guy's thinking about mountain wildness was greatly influ-
enced by Aldo Leopold and his *A Sand County Almanac*, which
Guy saw as an unequivocal statement of conscience. Leopold will
last because we have barely begun to work out his ideas.

I would like to think that Guy helped carry those ideas a
notch further. He believed it was essential to the health of our
human souls to retain the wildness in mountains. Being intangible—more a perception than anything else—wildness is far more
fragile than alpine flowers, the boot damage to which we can
measure, monitor, and attempt to control.

Wildness is imperceptibly eroded away. It is chipped at over
time by those who want to build a hut at a quiet view spot, or
locate a trail up a hitherto pathless ridge, or construct a bridge
where none had been deemed necessary in the past, or are overly
hasty in their use of helicopters in the mountains, or in traveling in

large groups, or in whipping out their cell phones, and on and on. These can be good things (except for possibly the cell phones!) or not. Each must be carefully weighed; measured against what is gained and what is lost in terms of mountain solitude and wildness. Wildness, it seems, is expendable. But once spent, like time itself, we can rarely gain it back.

Guy believed people shouldn't be preached at. He believed each of us should arrive at our own conclusions. He believed if we all came to the mountains in the spirit of having the peace and health of the wild mountains foremost in our minds, we would do the right things naturally.

Is this possible? Can we do the right things by the mountains? Can we preserve the spirit of wildness?

It seemed simple to Guy.

It seemed perhaps hopeless to Dr. Seuss's Once-ler, who comes to understand that "Unless someone like you cares a whole awful lot, nothing is going to get better. It's not."

Conservationist Geza Teleki wrote: "Everything is less important. Career is less important. Science is less important. Fame is less important than doing the right thing when you're dealing with the natural environment."

Guy bought into that, heart and soul.

On February 6th, Guy climbed to a place as familiar as home, his adored Franconia Ridge, to meet his own death. He found arctic cold and intemperate winds. He embraced an ample measure of wildness. Sometime in that subzero night he lay down the torch of his own igniting.

Other souls, I fully believe, will pick it up. More and more. They have already begun.

Laura Waterman
March 2000

Foreword

THE WATERMANS' COMPELLING NEW BOOK—concerned with preserving the wildness in wilderness—concentrates a half century of growing doubts about the success of wilderness protection programs in the United States. The second thoughts began almost as soon as the ink dried on law or proclamation designating an area "wilderness." What really had been accomplished other than putting a line on a map? Was wildness so fragile a quality that it might be destroyed even in a designated wilderness?

At the heart of this paradox is the fact that wilderness is not so much a place, but a *feeling* about one. In the first edition of *Wilderness and the American Mind* (1967) I defined wilderness as just as much a state of mind as a condition of geography. As such it could not only be developed to death but loved to death as well. This was a disturbing realization. Wilderness could be threatened by its friends as well as its traditional enemies. Even state-of-the-art minimum-impact wilderness travelers like the Watermans were part of the problem just as a consequence of their presence.

I may have also been among the first to point out the threat to wilderness posed by its own guardians. In the late 1970s in a lecture in Idaho in honor of Frank Church, I argued that wilderness management was a contradiction in terms. How do you go about controlling what is in essence the uncontrolled? But management of wild places has become the price of their existence, an unpleasant necessity. The reason, of course, is popularity. The supreme irony of the wilderness movement over the last century is that its very objectives have been threatened by its success. Another way of looking at this is to realize that it is really not the wilderness that needs management (it has been doing quite well, after all, for a couple of billion years), but people.

Some essential defining qualities are probably gone from wilderness forever. Guy and Laura Waterman will never cut the track of an eastern timber wolf even on their way to relatively isolated places like Lake Wietelmann. And the grizzly is just a memory in most of the American West. These wild "deor" (the word meant "animal" in Old English) are gone and, in a sense, so is wild-deor-ness, the place of wild animals. Lois Chrisler was correct in her observation that without big wild animals, wilderness is merely scenery. But there are some wilderness attributes we can enhance. Solitude is one. We are in charge here because we are the problem. Many people cannot enjoy solitude together. We can limit our numbers. Limitation could come from within the wilderness-using public: self-restraint. More likely, solitude will be a function of difficulty of access as the Watermans demonstrate in the pages that follow. David Brower put it this way: the crowd diminishes according to the square of the distance from the nearest road and the cube of the elevation above it.

But what if more and more people are willing to pay the physical price for admission to wilderness? What if hordes start going to the White Mountains in the winter months to get away from the summer hordes? This is not inconceivable as civilization becomes more concentrated and less bearable. The popularity of wilderness will increase as its presence on the planet decreases. Quotas and permits are likely to become the norm under which people visit wilderness. Indeed they are already here. The waiting list for a non-commercial river trip into the wild backcountry of

Grand Canyon National Park is eight years long. Don't just show up in Yosemite National Park expecting to backpack down the John Muir Trail; you may not get a permit for a month! Of course, Muir would have been outraged, just as the Watermans are, at the thought of being turned away from a wilderness that has reached its carrying capacity. But the point is that times have changed. If wilderness is to exist very far into the 21st century, it will be because its friends are willing to accept restraint.

There is still another dimension to this problem that deserves mention. Wilderness has *nonhuman* significance. It does not exist for snowshoe trips or whitewater river expeditions. It would be important even if no humans ever visited. Wild places have intrinsic value as habitats for creatures with biotic rights equal to our own. Wilderness is a place where we leave Earth alone; in the last analysis it is a gesture of planetary modesty.

Roderick Frazier Nash
Professor of Environmental Studies and History
University of California Santa Barbara

Acknowledgments

Anyone wrestling with ideas about wilderness values owes much to discussions with friends who share the same basic concerns but offer somewhat different perspectives. Many have helped us to think about the wild. It is difficult to single out individuals, but one wants to try.

We are especially conscious of those gentle teachers and observers of the outdoors Ruth and Keith Smiley, and going back further, Dan and Virginia Smiley. We learned much about the appreciation of wildness from Bill Waterman and John Waterman.

We are equally appreciative of a rising generation whose allegiance to the wilderness ideals has encouraged and reassured us about the future. These are many, but let us mention at least a dozen: Nat Scrimshaw, Peter Crane, Rebecca Oreskes, John Dunn, Lars and Jen Botzojorns, Mark Dindorf and Nancy Ritger, Emily and Peter Benson, Doug Mayer, Chuck Wooster, and Jeanie Cooley.

For reviewing the manuscript and providing specific suggestions, the authors are thankful for the thoughtful and perceptive help of our "three wise men," Louis Cornell, Mike Gottscho, and Phil Levin; as well as Bruce and Doreen Bolnick, Brian T. Fitzgerald, Edwin Ketchledge, Allen Koop, Chuck Kukla, Nat

Scrimshaw, Steve Smith, and Susan Staples. As always, Ned Therrien of the White Mountain National Forest was reliably helpful in providing information we needed.

Certain material herein has been adapted from earlier published form, and we are grateful to the original sources for allowing these adaptations. Thanks are due to Henry Wheelwright and Stone Wall Press in regard to chapters 16 and 18 and the case study "Winter above Treeline," which appeared substantially in the first edition of *Backwoods Ethics* (1979); to Mike Pogodzinski for chapter 15 and the case study "A Night in Odell Gully," which appeared first in *New England Outdoors*; and to Sandy Stott for chapter 17, which appeared in an earlier form in *Appalachia*.

All the good people at The Countryman Press have been a pleasure to work with, and we thank them for their confidence in our message and their professional skill in producing this book. The cheerful and competent folk at Xpress Copy Center in Hanover, New Hampshire, have been consistently good to us.

Most of all we'd like to thank Brad Snyder, whose contributions to our thinking and to the specific improvement of our manuscript, as well as his heartening support of our basic ideas, is most especially valued.

Laura and Guy Waterman
East Corinth, Vermont

I

SOMETHING MORE THAN TREES AND ROCKS

1

Fay's Quandary

...to prolong the luxury of the forest to the
last possible moment.

CHARLES ERNEST FAY, "MOUNT PASSACONAWAY"

ABOUT 100 YEARS before the publication of this book, on October 7, 1891, Professor Charles Ernest Fay of Tufts University read a paper before a gathering of Boston's 15-year-old Appalachian Mountain Club. In that faded document of a century ago lies a text suitable for thinking about today.

The Little Professor

Professor Fay was a small but spry climber who loved the wild side of the mountains. As a young man he went overseas for the usual summer climbing seasons in the Alps, obligatory for aspiring alpinists of his day. But when he got back home, he would head for the White Mountains of New Hampshire. There he seemed to find more genuine mountain wildness in the little-known corners of these forested hills. During the 1870s and 1880s, before there were a lot of hiking trails in the White Mountains, Professor Fay delved into many a hidden ravine and thrashed through thickets to many a summit where few had been before. Where difficulties lay, there he was happiest.

When trails were built in those hills, he turned to the Canadian Rockies for adventure. In that wilderness of unclimbed peaks, beginning when nearly the age of 50, he made explorations and first ascents of such notable summits as Victoria, Lefroy, and Dawson. Highly respected by his contemporaries, he served several terms (which was unusual) as president of both the Appalachian Mountain Club and the American Alpine Club, the dominant mountain societies of that generation. Canada named a good-sized mountain after him.

The bespectacled and bewhiskered face that peers out at us from faded old mountaineering journal photos conveys a spirit of humor as well as adventure. Most 19th-century visages look grim today. Who would want to go hiking with Ulysses Grant or Johannes Brahms? But Professor Fay is someone you'd want to have known, to have strolled a leaf-strewn trail with, to have joined as he sits on the barren scree slopes of Mount Lefroy sipping a cup of tea before making the first ascent.

Just before he went west, Professor Fay stood face to face with a quandary. We are fortunate that he aired his feelings in that paper read to the AMC gathering in Boston 100 years ago.

The Quandary

Fay's quandary was met on Mount Passaconaway, a graceful 4,060-foot wooded summit, the highest point in the Sandwich Range, that southernmost tier of the White Mountains. Fay first knew Passaconaway as a trailless mystery, "gloomy and ponderous." "In my youth it seemed to me of massive iron," he recalled, and was suffused with "the interest which attaches to the unknown." Until the summer of 1891 "it may be doubted whether a score of persons had ever found their way to its summit."

A few weeks after his second climb of this peak, a tumultuous wind broke over the region, concentrating its fury on the upper slopes of Passaconaway. The open woods that Fay had enjoyed became a "wreckage" of downed timber. The difficulty of reaching the top following that windstorm, combined with a local campaign to build more hiking trails, persuaded Professor Fay to cut a trail to the top of Mount Passaconaway.

After fruitless reconnaissances of other possibilities, Fay's party elected to start the trail at the end of an abandoned wood road to a deserted sawmill, "Dicy's" (today rendered "Dicey's Mill"). Not only did they cut a trail, with considerable difficulty in scouting the route through the upper-elevation blowdown, but they also erected a simple log shelter, 9 by 14 feet, 7 feet high in front sloping to 3 in back, and heaped inside with fragrant hemlock boughs. (Today you don't see hemlock anywhere near that high on the peak; perhaps the boughs were balsam fir? Professor Fay's field was Romance languages, not botany.)

At the end of several days' hard work, Professor Fay stood back to admire the handiwork of their "Passaconaway Lodge" and to contemplate the new-cut trail, which now made the once "gloomy and ponderous" peak into "a comfortable one day's trip for such as had no more time to devote to it." He recalled: "The sun was flooding all this with evening glory as we finished our work."

Surely this scene was cause for deep satisfaction, a rich sense of accomplishment, of opening up that lovely mountainside to be shared by such as had never been there before.

And yet...at this point Professor Fay began to reflect. What had they done?

> Was it justifiable to love the mountain not less, but climbers more? As one of the limited number to whom its secrets had been revealed, was it or not a breach of confidence to plan for the wholesale invasion of its privacy, and to aid in making it a readily accessible peak?

He thought of the wood road to the site of Dicy's mill, which local folks had promised to upgrade to provide easier access to the base of the new trail. "Another season will no doubt see a carriage-road as far as 'Dicy's'," he mused mournfully. "May no season ever see it carried farther; for whoever would not prefer to go from there to the summit by his own effort is not worthy to set foot on Passaconaway."

He thought of the viewpoints that had been cleared on the wooded summit—one on the east side, cut by another early bush-whacker, Frank Bolles, "whose love of wild nature had now and then led him to this secluded spot," and one on the northwest, cut by his own party. On the true summit, others had thought to clear a southward view by "much labor and ruthless destruction of fine trees," but Fay had prevailed on them to desist, and instead to select "a tall spruce with branches conveniently set for climbing," which they furnished with "an improvised ladder." If anyone needed a view from the very top, let them exert the added effort and ingenuity of climbing another 15 feet for it. Leave the trees alone. They were there first. They live there, we just visit. Professor Fay, though he seemed not to know the difference between hemlock and balsam fir, believed that trees had rights too.

By the light, first, of a dwindling campfire and, later, of a harvest moon, Professor Fay sat up all night at Camp Passaconaway. "It was too glorious a night to sleep." Perhaps he was seeking, in the novelist Ellen Glasgow's words, "to preserve, within a wild sanctuary, an inaccessible valley of reveries."

In the morning they broke camp, the party fully expecting to descend with pride their new-cut trail. Instead Professor Fay announced they would bushwhack down over the Wonalancet Ridge. Back into the jumble of blowdown, over the uneven mossy terrain of rocks and downed logs, and on down the steep slope, the puzzled party followed the intrepid Charles Ernest Fay.

What's Going On Here?

Why the bushwhack down? Wrote Fay in his paper before the AMC: "To prolong the luxury of the forest to the last possible moment."

That is a fine sensibility which finds "luxury" in the untamed forest, not the cleared path; in the difficult way, not the easy; the road less traveled by, which makes all the difference. Would that we could have tripped behind Professor Fay as he thrashed through the thickets and down the Wonalancet Ridge, disdaining the new-cut trail that he himself had conceived and directed 100 years ago.

What was Fay doing? Can we learn from him?

On one level, the answer is that Professor Fay was savoring the yet-untamed wildness of the mountain. In spite of the new trail and the sheltering roof, the mountain's wildness remained yet untamed, providing only that those who valued that wildness would seek it out. That was his message to his puzzled companions in the 1890s, and it is equally Professor Fay's message to us in the 1990s. Our mountains have many more trails and many more sheltering roofs than Professor Fay's did; but we can yet preserve that spirit of wildness, provided that we value that wildness, savor it, and do what we must to preserve it for the 1990s and the 2090s as well.

But, as Professor Fay recognized in warning against extending the carriage road beyond Dicy's and in ruling against cutting summit trees, that wildness is fragile. We can lose it, we can be agents of its destruction, if we are not wise and caring stewards. The key is to decide where our values lie. It is fun to enjoy the easy trail and the sheltering roof. But if we indulge ourselves too much in bringing civilized comforts, do we not destroy qualities that originally brought us to the mountain? Is it not better to savor the wildness, to throw ourselves into the very uncomfortableness of the untamed thickets, to "prolong the luxury of the forest"?

Professor Fay wanted to share the mountain experience: that's why he built the trail and shelter on Passaconaway and that's why he helped form and lead the Appalachian Mountain Club. But he also recognized that the essence of the mountain experience is challenge, difficulty, reaching the inaccessible, rising to heights you hadn't achieved before. When he mused over the results of his work on Passaconaway, he was contemplating an important question: Just what is it we're trying to share? The experience of being on top of the mountain? Or the experience of climbing to get there and *then* being there, in an altogether richer spirit? Do we really do anyone favors by smoothing the way? Or, in our patronizing, self-aggrandizing role as trail builder and shelter provider, do we impoverish the mountain experience for those we set out to help?

What values matter most to us? In an increasingly urbanized society, surrounded by technological marvels in our everyday lives, why do we value the mountains? Are they a sanctuary where we preserve a special kind of experience to savor? Or are they merely a recreational gymnasium for our off-hours? Aren't they something more?

Half a century later, and 100 miles to the west, another who loved to share the mountains, Russell M. L. Carson of the Adirondacks, expressed his concern:

> In all our thinking about recreational development, we ought constantly to remember that wilderness and natural beauty are the real charm of the Adirondacks, and that preservation is as much our objective as helping more people to share our joy in them.

Professor Fay sought to preserve, to savor, and he set an example to his companions and to us. As trail builder and hiker, he sought the right balance between sharing and preserving. He built the trail, but he urged no carriage road. He cut an outlook, but he required his summit visitor to climb a bit more (on that spruce with "conveniently set" branches) to see the view. He took satisfaction in the trail and shelter he'd built, but when he had thought about it, he elected to descend by a pathless way "to prolong the luxury of the forest to the last possible moment."

2

What Are We Trying to Preserve?

*"Would you tell me, please, which way I ought
to go from here?"
"That depends a good deal on where you want to get to,"
said the Cat.
"I don't much care where—" said Alice.
"Then it doesn't matter which way you go," said the Cat.*

LEWIS CARROLL, *ALICE IN WONDERLAND*

WHAT PROFESSOR FAY wrestled with on Mount Passaconaway in 1891, we all confront today. What are we building? What are we trying to preserve? What is happening to our backcountry?

The underlying question 100 years later, not only in the Sandwich Range or the White Mountains, and not just through these United States, but in varied forms throughout the surface of this crowded globe, is whether the spirit of wildness is facing its "last possible moment." The question is whether, and specifically *how*, we may prolong the "luxury" of having the quality of mountain experience that Professor Fay knew and loved so well.

Fay's quandary is ours. He was ahead of his time in acknowledging it. We are tardy—we hope, not too late—in failing to recognize it today.

Fay's Quandary 100 Years Later

So far things could have been a lot worse. As a nation of frontier settlers, we have done much better than might have been expected of us: We've set aside magnificent tracts of wild scenery in the form of national and state parks and forests. Many well-to-do private sources have reserved extensive acreage to be kept in a natural state. As early as 1964—which is really remarkably early when you consider that the back-to-the-land sentiment didn't well up until the later 1960s—Congress passed the Wilderness Act. That meant a political majority perceived broad support for preserving substantial areas "where the earth and its community of life are untrammeled by man."

Today there are a lot of people out there who'd like to trammel the heck out of that land. The idea that land should be kept undisturbed—or "locked up," as the trammelers put it—is being sharply questioned. Loggers, who correctly point out that we all want forest products in our lives (paper, furniture, wooden houses) and that trees are a renewable resource, would like to cut anything they can lay a chainsaw to. Families in the Pacific Northwest display signs reading "This Family Supported by the Timber Industry." Well-heeled organizations lobby for mineral and energy production on all kinds of federal land, including national parks and wilderness areas.

Nor is the threat to natural land confined to loggers and strip miners and oil drillers. Much land that stood in a natural state for generations of private ownership is now changing hands fast, and a lot of good people want to buy second-home lots on that land. These are not insensitive slobs who will toss beer cans in the woods. These people are a lot like you and us. They like nature: that's why they want to own a piece of scenic "unspoilt" country-side. "A conservationist," defines the conservationist Bradley Snyder, "is a person who just built *his* house in the woods."

The cause of wilderness, of wildness, is poorly served by rhetoric that portrays the despoilers as wealthy, greedy corpora-tions, looking only at the bottom line. A lot of little folk make their living logging, and they love the woods. A lot of good people want to own a chunk of those big forests, and part of a mountain they'd like even better.

Besides, we recreationists increasingly prove the truth in the old song, we always hurt the ones we love, the ones we shouldn't hurt at all. Western trail riders on their beloved horses are chewing up popular trails mercilessly, leaving mushy quagmires of mud, with a generous interlarding of horse manure. All-terrain vehicles leave their remorseless tracks in formerly pristine haunts. The voracious demands of the ski "industry" threaten to devour, for recreational development, yet more mountains, yet more now-undeveloped forest lands. Concessionaires seek to convert each national park into a sort of Disney attraction, measuring results by the volume of "people moved."

Striking yet closer to home, too many of us hikers and climb-ers rationalize a long list of impositions on the spirit of wildness, in the form of facilities, trails, technological supports like radios and helicopters, large parties of students or others we'd like to intro-duce to the outdoors. We defend our practices in the name of sharing the mountain experience, or managing backcountry resources better, or ensuring "user" safety, or building a political base for the support of wilderness. Roderick Nash concluded his landmark study *Wilderness and the American Mind* with the observa-tion:

> The problem is that dams, mines, and roads are not the basic threat to the wilderness quality of an environment. People are, and whether they come with economic or recreational motives is, in a sense, beside the point.

Often the end result of too many hikers is little distinguishable from the effects of the all-terrain vehicle or of the developer; a loss of wildness, the incursion of a civilizing presence, the desecration of the province of the mountain gods, a failure to "prolong the luxury of the forest" as Professor Fay understood it.

Body and Soul

Preserving the spirit of wildness requires action on at least two entirely distinguishable fronts. In the first place, the more obvious forms of destruction—industrialization, whether by miners or the recreation industry or second-home developers—must be fended off from significant blocs of natural lands. But after that, we must decide what we're preserving that land for: the preserved land must be treated with respect for its wild character, its internal integrity, the spirit of the land.

The former action seems to be the glamour side of the wilderness cause. It gets a lot of attention and support, and we thank the Lord for that. We lose a lot of land here and there, but we also preserve a lot; and we hope the big guns who are leading this fight for all of us will continue to win. To do so they need all of our support. We salute all the efforts, by groups as varied as the low-key Nature Conservancy to the high-pitched Earth First!, to protect large tracts of wilderness.

But we want to ask you to look for a moment beyond those land preservation campaigns, to ask essentially the question that troubled Professor Fay: Once we have "saved" the land, how do we preserve the spirit of wildness out there in the woods, up there on the heights?

It is this second front, the less dramatic and more subtle issue, that we address in these pages. Can we develop a higher respect for the innate character of wild land and of the wilderness experience? Can we protect both the quality of the human experience obtainable in wilderness and, more basic, the integrity of the natural processes that define it as wilderness? Can we reverse the civilizing momentum and reclaim a touch of wildness even on land that appeared lost to the development or recreation mania? Is a concerned consensus possible that will leave islands of wildness left in a world overly dominated by humanity?

Those questions suggest the need for, in Aldo Leopold's oft-quoted phrase, a new land ethic, in relation specifically to wild land. Some rough-hewn wilderness ethic is needed in our time, just as a general land ethic was needed in Leopold's and remains needed today.

Elsewhere we have addressed some of the issues involved in preserving the physical attributes of wildness—the trees, the soils, the waters, the constituent physical elements of the backcountry and the mountain environment. This physical environment is the sine qua non of the backcountry experience. There is no point in worrying about spiritual considerations if we do not first preserve the green woods, the lofty crags, the hushed desert, the pure waters, the quiet valleys, the windswept ridges…the moss on the boulder…the raven on the cloud…the frost feathers on the summit cairn…the varicolored rocks beneath the clear pool…the star flower at trail's edge. If you want to pursue that important part of the picture, you may want to look over our *Backwoods Ethics: Environmental Issues for Hikers and Campers*.

But to us an equally vital and even more fragile and threatened part of the picture is the spiritual side of wildness, the intangibles, the subjective elements. In these pages we invite you to think with us about these intangibles, the spiritual side of wild.

Matters of Approach

We do not propose to lead you through a profound philosophical exploration of theoretical issues. Perhaps someone should write that book, but we're not the ones to do it. Profound theorists we are not. We're just two people who spend a lot of time in the woods and on the mountains; who have observed a few things and asked ourselves a few questions about wildness; and who would like to invite you to share our thoughts and think about some practical questions yourself.

> What are we trying to preserve?
> What are the threats to the *wild*ness in wilderness?
> What can we do about it?

We want to emphasize two matters of approach that you'll find recurring throughout the pages of this book. First, you won't find answers to these or other tough questions here. In fact, Fay's quandary is precisely that: a quandary, a logistical cul-de-sac, a clash of interior values, and there is no fully satisfying answer. The clash of wilderness preservation versus use and enjoyment by thousands is inherently unresolvable. But that does not absolve any of us from striving to resolve it, from doing the best our generation can to preserve the spirit of wildness.

Second, where reasonable people may have divergent but deeply held opinions, the most important element in fruitful discussion is respect for other viewpoints. We're speaking here of genuine respect, good-humored recognition that maybe we haven't thought each move through adequately, and perhaps the other person (who is obviously wrong, pig-headed, perverse!) may have a legitimate viewpoint after all. The subtle point is to hold deep convictions and to care strongly, yet to acknowledge that others may also.

The purpose of this book is not to get you to agree with a program or philosophy of ours, but to try to help us all to think about issues that matter.

Like Professor Fay, we must sit up all night and think. And in the morning, we must take action "to prolong the luxury of the forest to the last possible moment."

3

What Is the Wild?

The best in nature, like the best in art, is sacred. Look upon it respectfully, reverentially, or not at all. Even the wild beasts know that much.

JOAQUIN MILLER,
GAME REGIONS OF THE UPPER SACRAMENTO (1888)

THE BACKWOODS ETHICS agenda of the 1970s responded largely to blatant physical problems. Campsites were dying, trails were eroding. Up above treeline alpine flowers were being trampled. On the rock climber's cliffs, piton cracks were disintegrating before our eyes. Most of the concerned reaction focused on saving the physical resources of the mountain world—the rocks, trees, clear-flowing waters, alpine tundra.

During the 1990s more and more voices are being raised about something more than the physical resources. Increasingly we notice that even the once-bureaucratic old US Forest Service seems unashamed now to talk openly about the spiritual side of the forest experience. Wilderness, says the USFS Rocky Mountain Regional Office, is

> a location for renewal of mind and spirit. This rejuvenation is more than what might occur from simply withdrawing or

escaping from urban pressures. What makes the wilderness experience unique is the tranquility, peace, and silence to be found in the wilderness and the opportunity it affords for contemplation.

The spirit of wilderness, or more generally of wildness, involves intangibles. In several significant ways, the wildness of wilderness is being violated by means that do no serious environmental harm, if we perceive the environment in strictly physical terms. Without underestimating for a moment the importance of physical preservation, we venture the opinion that the intangible or spiritual side of wilderness and wildness is also important—and even more in jeopardy.

Edward Abbey is not necessarily our favorite writer, much less our folk hero. His abrasive style rubs a lot of people wrong, and wilderness needs allies from groups for whom Abbey showed conspicuous contempt. Abbey struck some points right on the head with his hard-hitting approach, however, and one simile of his is especially striking:

> We have agreed not to drive our automobiles into cathedrals, concert halls, art museums, legislative assemblies, private bedrooms and the other sanctums of our culture; we should treat our national parks with the same deference, for they, too, are holy places.

Amen! Wilderness areas are like cathedrals, and there are some things you just don't do in cathedrals. You don't drive a dirt bike there; you don't play a radio; you don't fly a helicopter up the nave to the chancel, even if that would be an efficient way to supply wine and wafers for each Sunday's "users"; you don't mark the aisles with plastic ribbon to find your pew or to note where the carpet needs repair; you don't bring a voluble party of 25 friends. Notice that none of these outrageous acts would physically mar the cathedral. But they outrage the spirit of the place. That is what those who reverence wilderness values feel is the needed approach to the woods and hills.

In later chapters we want to invite you to consider several specific ways in which wilderness values are being undermined, in which the sense of stewardship is going unheeded, and in which a casual and uncaring betrayal of the spirit of wildness is slipping into the woods and hills, where it doesn't belong.

Before we get into specifics, though, let's take a few minutes to think about what it is we're trying to preserve. What is wildness?

Our dictionary lists a number of meanings of that word, many of them relevant to this discussion:

- living or growing in its original natural state
- not normally domesticated or cultivated
- not civilized
- unruly, rough, lawless
- violently disturbed, turbulent, stormy

"Its original natural state"? Much of the movement to preserve wildness is simply an effort to hold on to a nature-dominated world against the incursions of a humanity-dominated world, with its machines, its bustle, its glories, its malaise. To safeguard trees and moss and wind and mist and white-throated sparrows. To walk away from computers and airports, yes, and also from French cuisine and Mozart sonatas. To let nature be. John Van Dyke called deserts "the breathing places of the west," and that nice phrase is apt for mountains and polar wastes and open seas—all the wild places left on this overcivilized planet, places where the natural world has room to breathe.

In a broadly conceived discussion of these issues, the lyrical writer Gary Snyder reminds us:

Thoreau says "give me a wildness no civilization can endure." That's clearly not difficult to find. It is harder to imagine a civilization that wildness can endure, yet this is just what we must try to do.... We need a civilization that can live fully and creatively together with wildness.

In another place Thoreau called wilderness "a civilization other than our own." He may have had in mind the intricate order and efficiency of nature. We prefer to avoid the word "civilization" completely, to think of the natural world as a distinctly *separate* compartment, a biosphere dominated by natural rather than human-initiated forces, the realm distinctively separate *from* civilization.

Today articulate voices question whether a truly natural world still exists. A powerful case can be made that the natural world has been so altered, polluted, "improved," and otherwise imposed upon, that all we have left are scattered token reminders of a lost world, preserved at our sufferance for the gratification of our sentimental reveries.

In a slim but eloquent book called *The End of Nature*, the Adirondacks writer Bill McKibben has marshaled the evidence that no part of the world is exempt from the influences of civilization now. Not only can humanity go anywhere it chooses—and does—but we've acidified *all* the planet's rainfall, drained our pollutants into *all* the seven seas, and done things to the ozone layer and otherwise distorted the contents of the atmosphere over *all* the globe—so much so that there is no truly natural world left. Our industrialization, our technosphere, dominates the once-imperturbable biosphere. Now it is human interference that accounts for the major trends in the world's evolution.

Other writers such as Barry Commoner have issued similar warnings. Wendell Berry writes despairingly: "Nothing now exists anywhere on earth that is not under threat of human destruction. Poisons are everywhere. Junk is everywhere." Noel Perrin has found a vivid metaphor for the human dilemma that confronts us:

> We are like goldfish who have been living in an aquarium for as long as we can remember; and being clever goldfish, we have discovered how to manipulate the controls of the aquarium: put more oxygen in the water, get rid of the pesky turtle we never liked anyway, triple the supply of goldfish food. Only once we realize we're partly running the aquarium, it scares some of us. What if we make a mistake, and wreck the aquarium entirely? We couldn't live outside it.

We tend to a guarded optimism. Certainly we have overloaded the environment with our arrogant technologies. But nature is too resilient an antagonist to be easily vanquished. The natural world still has power, immensity, complexity, beauty beyond humanity's power either to create or to manipulate. What various kinds of wilderness have in common, whether mountain or ocean or polar ice or desert sands, is a vivid sense of both the overpowering strength and the delicate intricacy of nature, and its importance relative to the simplistic dullness, even insignificance, of us people. Maybe that doesn't quite put it right. Let's try again: the immensity, the vitality, the grandeur, the wonder and mystery of the natural world, against which mere humans are exposed as utterly frail and insignificant. These are qualities of a world that tests us, a world in which, if we take it on its own terms and measure ourselves truly against it, we find that small and frail as we are, we are capable of rising to heights of experience and performance; that even one puny human can be vital and alive, wonderful and mysterious. We are, in such cases, learning a lot about the spirit of the natural world, but also, through the natural world, about the spirit of humankind: ourselves.

Martin Luther, someone claims, said something to the effect that if he knew the world were to end tomorrow, he would plant an apple tree today. It is the cry of many concerned critics of the social imperative, and the theme of this book, that we should continue to preserve islands of wilderness, and then we should work hard to preserve the *wildness* in that wilderness. We must recognize what wildness is and honor it, rather than belittle it by flexing our interventionist muscles.

Is it a losing battle? If it is, humanity will be among the losers.

Nature is born wild and should remain forever so. We are born with wildness in our natures, which must succumb to civilizing if we are to dwell in society. But that residue of wildness in us responds to the wildness in nature's world. That is one reason why we seek and long for wildness. It is a good enough reason to try to preserve the cathedral of the wild.

4

The Spiritual Side of Wild

Without a sense of the unknown and unknowable,
life is flat and barren.

JOHN BURROUGHS

WHAT ELSE is wildness? Certain attributes come to mind:
remoteness, inaccessibility, uncertainty, mystery. A wild place can
be a difficult place, uncomfortable for humans. And we should seek
to keep it that way, not try to make it safer, more comfortable,
more like the civilization we leave behind.

On one level, a true wilderness experience requires vast tracts
of land where the ways of humanity are banished miles and miles
away; whole riversheds and mountain ranges where you'll meet
neither road nor building, and few other people either; a time
commitment such that returning to civilization would take at least
a full day, better more. A dark illimitable country without bound,
without dimension, where length, breadth, and height and time
and place are lost.

But is sheer size an essential condition of wildness? We argue
that it is a useful, a very useful, but not an essential condition,
though we have to feel a little uncomfortable about that position.

We do believe that you can find wildness just a couple of miles off the trail if you work at it, and if all of us resist the easy ways to encroach upon such opportunities. In fact, a large part of the purpose of this book is to plead, with all the force we can muster, for preserving the spirit of wildness in the little places where it still exists. But we simply have to concede that wildness on a small scale is a very, very fragile concept. If you can walk out of it in an hour or two, is it wild? We *think* so. But it's close, we grant.

Once recently we visited one of the most interesting work-places in the world: the summit weather observatory on Mount Washington in winter. The world's highest winds have been recorded here—more precisely, the world's fastest observed natural, land-surface winds. The combination of these winds, plus cold, plus the severe storms, plus the erratic changeability, combine to make this the "world's worst weather." Since a friend of ours happens to work as one of the world's worst weather observers, we had the privilege of sharing that unique world up there for a few days.

On one wild stormy winter day we ventured out of the tiny island of calm that the interior of the observatory constitutes, with the purpose of going to climb a neighboring peak. We won't trouble you with the temperature and wind data other than to assure you that both were formidable. A crucial point was the low visibility. As we battled our way through the shrieking, buffeting winds and blowing ice crystals, we concentrated intently on keeping in touch with an indifferently maintained line of cairns, much of them shrouded in such thick rime ice as to fade into the whirring white mist unnoticed. It was grand adventure just to struggle a bit over a mile and a bit over 1,000 feet of descent, a few hundred feet of ascent, then return the way we had come.

The consequences of a mistake should be understood. Had we lost contact with those cairns we would have been cast adrift in a featureless, directionless fog of hostile elements, with a limited time span for survival, given the wind, temperature, and other conditions. Once out of touch with your path, your options would suddenly be few and unattractive. Going blindly downhill into the trees would eventually protect you from the wind but really constitute no feasible alternative, as the first belt of trees to be reached would be that stunted forest of krummholz, so impenetrable and, in a thick snow cover, indecipherable as to reduce progress to a snail's pace. Going back uphill till you reach the summit building sounds a bit easier than it is, because the mountain is not a simplistic cone but a jumble of boulder piles covered with snow and rime. If you lost your bearings you could well be, as the cliché has it, unable to tell which way is up. Besides, all rational plans and procedures are shaken to pieces by the perpetual battering and noise of that wind and driving ice. Without that tenuous grip on that line of cairns, the world is a meaningless chaos of whiteness. Remember that chapter in *Moby Dick* where Melville argues that, of all colors, pure white is the most ominous, the most hostile, a color in which "there yet lurks an elusive something…which strikes more of panic to the soul than the redness which affrights in blood"?

We bring all this up because of the vivid sensation we experienced as the wind-racked shroud of thick ice fog closed behind us, obliterating our visual contact with the summit observatory and its cluster of buildings. Especially as we took compass bearings and groped ahead to chart our uncertain course, always gripped with the thought that we must not lose track of where we were, it became palpable that here was wildness. No vast tract of forest— indeed, scarce 100 yards away lay a quiet carpeted interior with comfortable chairs and good friends—yet the slightest mistake or inattention to the details of our itinerary and we could well have been adrift in a featureless maelstrom of white. Such a mistake could have been literally life-threatening.

Such experiences convince us that, at least at one level, true wildness certainly does not require large space. It does require commitment to a situation where wild nature is in charge, where tiny humanity is exposed to genuine risk, where the deck is not stacked in our favor but the wild gods of nature hold all the aces.

Wildness can take milder forms than a winter storm, yet still be found in a small setting. On one Labor Day weekend we found ourselves oppressed with the sense of overcrowding on the popular trails and celebrated summits. So we selected a peak with a reputation as being the least "interesting" of the higher summits in the area. To call it a peak is shameless flattery; it is just a shapeless mound that happens to rise to an elevation that puts it on the peakbaggers' lists. We figured that few people would go there, even on Labor Day, and those that did would use the trail. So we chose a different, off-trail route. For a couple of hours we picked our way slowly uphill through a tangle of downed trunks, uneven footing, and trees of diminishing height. As we laboriously crested the summit ridge, we found a fold in the terrain where we dropped on the turf to catch our breath and sit a bit. Gradually we became intensely conscious of the little piece of the world we occupied: a cleft in a forested mountainside, our vista hemmed in to less than 100 feet in all directions. With no distant distractions, we grew vividly aware of our world of greens, grays, browns, and an infinity of shadings between. Here were ferns and sorrel and moss and lichened trunks that knew no world of people. We were guests in a room unaccustomed to company. We heard the eloquent silence. Here was an aspect of wildness that in its way was as impressive as that hostile white world of winter above treeline. Yet, as up there, we were not far, physically, from the world of other people. Here, on Labor Day weekend, we were not five miles from a parking lot jammed with cars and humanity. Within two miles in every direction were trails on which you would not go 10 minutes without seeing another party. But here, up in that little green cleft of a ridge that most hikers spurn as not being "interesting," we sat in a little island of wildness.

Remoteness is not necessarily measured in miles. One can be remote from civilization's clutches and crutches in a short space and a brief time.

Whether large-scale or small, an essential attribute of wildness is remoteness, inaccessibility. Some plead for easier access to wilderness. Isn't that confusing the point? The essence of wildness is difficulty of access.

Difficulty? This is a highly variable concept. One person's challenging climb is another's Sunday stroll. Notes Roderick Nash, "The Yukon trapper would consider a trip to northern Minnesota a return to civilization, while for the vacationer from Chicago it is a wilderness adventure indeed." Thus for all seeking the experience of wildness in the mountains, an essential element is challenge. If you didn't have to rise a bit to meet some testing of yourself, physical or psychic, don't claim a wilderness experience.

Mystery? Countless times we've noticed some odd unexplained divergence in nature's pattern: a patch of inactive vegetation in an otherwise lush ridge side, for example. We also notice that certain of our friends, upon having this phenomenon pointed out, instinctively offer an explanation for the seemingly aberrant occurrence. To a lot of people, it seems important to identify positively *why* everything is as it is. In truth, we often find these explanations unconvincing, a bit labored, or possibly inapplicable to what we see in the terrain just a few yards further on. We, like some others we know, are thoroughly content to leave nature's little caprice unexplained.

The poet John Keats, seeking to explain the greatness of Shakespeare, observed that, unlike many writers, the Bard was capable of diving deep into his characters, yet wisely left much unexplained. Shakespeare, said Keats, "is capable of being in uncertainties, mysteries, doubts, without any irritable reaching after fact and reason." Just so proceed most careful observers of the natural world.

That quiet philosopher of the land, Wendell Berry, speaks of his recurring experience in going to the woods:

> One has come into the presence of mystery. After all the trouble one has taken to be a modern man, one has come back under the spell of a primitive awe, wordless and humble.

We could not prove it, but we suspect that mystery is an essential element of wildness. This is what Professor Fay called, with his generation's delicate understatement, "the interest which attaches to the unknown." Earlier, Fay's contemporary, the novelist George MacDonald, observed:

> Things that cannot be explained so widen the horizon around us! open to us fresh regions for questions and answer, for possibility and delight!

If we understand everything in what we see in the natural world, can we fully lose ourselves in the wildness of any scene? Are not some matters better hid? Should we not be filled with a sense of wonder? Do we need to know all that the great Architect did wisely to conceal, and not divulge his secrets to be scanned by those who ought rather admire?

We need a significant level of mystery in the world around us. That is an essential attribute of wildness.

With the mystery comes a consciousness of the scale of nature, its intricacy, or the genius of its interrelationships, or its raw power, or its subtlety. All these intense impressions send a message about our own limitations. The mountain world (or that of the desert, or the sea, or the polar regions) is so much more impressive than the proudest achievements of humanity, so much more powerful, more beautiful, more important.

The Minnesota tramper Peter Leschak captured the awe that wildness conveys in describing an early trip in the uplands of Colorado's San Juan Mountains wilderness:

> Suddenly I felt small. Too small. That infinite, expressionless sky would have swallowed a shout or scream like a drop dissolving in the ocean. I tried turning to an imaginary companion, tried to talk to the friends of memory, but the ancient rocks froze my thoughts with their stony silence. This wilderness didn't need me, didn't want me—I was mortal, green, and far too new to command respect or even recognition from it.

And yet, viewed in right relation to this natural world, we can find humanity's efforts ennobled and ennobling. If we try to cope with a winter storm above treeline, we soon know our place, to use the language of intimidation. But if we do cope with that storm without too much loss of control or dignity—if we marshal all our strength, composure, knowledge painfully extracted from many experiences in other storms, concentration, courage, unflapped persistence with details, all those qualities that the unforgiving pressures of that storm ruthlessly demand from us—and if we come down off the mountain, perhaps a bit bewildered, battered, bemused, and more than a bit cold and exhausted, we feel a sense of achievement, an exhilaration of self, that few other experiences in life afford.

We have not, of course, beaten the storm or conquered the mountain. Nature has convincingly shown who's boss. We did, however, rise to greater heights within ourselves than we had thought we might. "Have we conquered an enemy?" asked George Leigh Mallory. "None but ourselves."

Nature remains untamed, "violently disturbed, turbulent, stormy," "unruly, rough, lawless," "not civilized."

What a sterile, empty world without this wild spirit at large! Is it not worth our best efforts to save?

5

Values in Conflict in the Backcountry

And I will learn what everything costs.
GEORGE ELIOT, *MIDDLEMARCH*

BEHOLD FOUR BRIEF vignettes, each set in one of the north-eastern forest states we happen to know best:

Scene 1
New York's Adirondacks: the popular trail to Lake Pristine. For long stretches, board plank walkways have been laid down over the wet trailbed. These are not the rough-hewn logs from the surrounding woods, but standardized two-inch lumber imported from valley suppliers.

The objective: to provide hikers with a dry-shod passage through mud patches, not so much for their convenience and comfort as to put an end to the trail-widening, vegetation-destroying effect of hikers skirting the mud in wet weather.

Continuing along the planks, we finally emerge from the trees to the shore of Lake Pristine. Here we head for the lakeside lean-to that we recall as being so idyllic in an earlier visit: Mobbed Shelter. At this now heavily used site, we note that wood railings have been erected to discourage hikers from cutting through the woods every which way.

The objective: to channel foot traffic in the area around Mobbed Shelter into certain paths only, thereby allowing forest vegetation to regenerate.

Curtain. On to the next scene.

Scene 2

Vermont's Green Mountains during Outdoor Weeks at Withitte School. Along a series of craggy, forested ridgelines, the entire senior class of Withitte School, almost 100 strong, is spending two weeks in November, dispersed in groups of 10 seniors plus two adult leaders, traveling largely off-trail and camping out every night. The students are taught tidbits of woodlore and forest ecology, but the main point is simply to be in the outdoors, to survive the sometimes harsh weather of Vermont's November, and to enjoy the camaraderie and mutual support of a backcountry expedition. There are 10 such groups, and this is the 24th year of Outdoor Weeks at Withitte.

The objective: to expose each senior to the wilderness experience; Withitte is a highly regarded school that combines excellence in the form of high academic standards with a broadly progressive concept of education.

Four days from the end of the program, each student goes on a "solo," spending three days in complete solitude in the woods. Most of them spend this time (remember, it's November in northern Vermont) keeping a small fire going. Each senior is supposed to record events and thoughts during these three days in a journal. They contemplate the surrounding woods or look inward at themselves. A nearby camp of adult leaders keeps its own fire going and has a system for unobtrusively checking on the safety of each individual without intruding on his or her solitude.

The objective: to give each senior the unique experience of three days of solitude, "perhaps the only time in their lives they'll ever have this experience," according to one Withitte faculty member.

On the last day of Outdoor Weeks the entire class climbs Mount Trampled, and the headmaster comes along to give an important address in this magnificent outdoor setting. The objective: to cap this priceless fortnight's experience in the wild.

Curtain, and on to the next scene.

Scene 3

New Hampshire's White Mountains. Fly-in day at Grandview Lodge. A helicopter drones in over the forest ridges carrying a netful of supplies—food, propane, trail equipment for sale to Grandview guests. In an opening in the trees behind the lodge, two college students working at Grandview this summer await the helicopter's arrival. A few visiting hikers rush out on the porch of the lodge to watch the helicopter hover at treetop level while the youths expertly swoop in and unhook the net, carry off the incoming load, and replace it with an outgoing load, the chief component of which is a half dozen extremely heavy 55-gallon drums, sealed very tight. Each of these drums had reposed beneath the seat of Grandview's indoor privy for a while; now full, they are destined for a landfill at a valley town below. His new load secure, the helicopter pilot waves cheerily to the ground crew and slowly lifts off and drones back over the forested ridges.

The objective: to supply food, fuel, and other wants to the guests of Grandview Lodge, so that these hikers can enjoy their hiking vacations without having to carry their own needs on their backs (heavy!); also (on the flight out) to prevent pollution of mountain waters by flying out human wastes in a safe, efficient manner.

Curtain. On to the final scene.

Scene 4

Maine's north woods. The front porch of a ranger station at Wonder State Park. A throng of 20 hikers mills about, awaiting the uncertain results of the morning's weather report. Finally, a neatly dressed ranger steps out and, with a friendly word, posts the day's judgment: good weather, and anyone is allowed to climb the mountain. The hikers rush off to find their packs and begin the day's ascent. Had the weather report been adverse, however, the ranger might have announced that no one would be allowed to climb the mountain that day. This is part of a comprehensive safety program, other parts of which have included a vigorous overblazing of trails; ranger inspection of hiker footgear, clothing, and equipment; an age limit for children; a certain time of day after which no one may start up the mountain; and strict registration of everyone in Wonder State Park, so that rangers know where every single visitor is every single night and whether they are safely down by dark.

The objective: to ensure the safety of each and every visitor to Wonder State Park.

Final Curtain

These four vignettes are fictional, but each closely parallels actual situations in our northeastern backcountry, and doubtless similar situations in forests and parks, mountains and deserts, throughout the continent.

The objectives served illustrate the diversity of values that shape management policies, public and private, and shape also the resulting experience available to backcountry hikers. Obviously, each objective is praiseworthy. In one or another of these four scenes, we see a dedication to several different underlying goals:

- Preserving forest resources from the damaging effects of hikers
- Exposing young people to the wilderness experience
- Providing access and facilities so that large numbers of people and a broad cross-section of the population may enjoy the mountains, not just the physically robust
- Limiting the environmental impact of these large numbers by concentrating overnight use in a closed facility and flying out human wastes
- Ensuring the safety of wilderness recreationists

Can anyone be *against* those goals? Anyone against motherhood? Country? Apple pie? Of course not. These are all genuinely desirable goals.

But obviously your authors have something in mind. What we would like to explore with you is the not-too-obscure point that good objectives sometimes come in conflict with other good objectives, especially in the backcountry.

How Much Is Too Much?

In scene 1 the objective is to protect that resource. Who can argue with that? No one can look at the environmental impact of the lug-soled army during the backpacking boom, the damage wrought on soils and delicate forest plant life, without wanting to see urgent measures taken to save the purely physical forest environment.

But some hikers are going to wonder about walking on planks of store-bought lumber for mile after mile. If you wanted to walk on a boardwalk during your vacation, you'd have gone to Atlantic City, not the Adirondacks. Others will wonder about being fenced in as they stroll the shores of Lake Pristine.

It must be conceded that elements have been introduced into the hiker's experience that have a taint of civilization and of regimentation about them, and that do some violence to the hiker's sense of being in backcountry.

How much is too much?

Partly it is a matter of management sensitivity to wilderness values, combined with a willingness to put a little extra effort into hiding the mailed fist in a kid glove. We have seen effective barriers around shelters in the form of dead trees or large stones, so positioned as to encourage traffic to walk in certain paths and not fan out everywhere. Steve Page, a trailworker during early efforts by the Appalachian Mountain Club to revegetate the camper-trampled woods around Liberty Springs in the White Mountains, discussed the options thus:

A large decaying log placed next to the trail parallel to it is an excellent barrier—both physically and visually.... Another less subtle barrier is the rock wall.... Split rail fences are a possibility for drastic no-access areas but somehow we must keep our backcountry from turning into a suburbia.

For muddy trails, split-log or topped-log bridges hewn from trees on-site—or better yet, large stones pried from the nearby mountainside—can provide solid footing with less intrusion than store-milled lumber.

An irony in some places is that zealous advocates of the formal "wilderness" designation have decreed rules against cutting live trees for any purpose, so that trail crews are required to use imported milled lumber instead of cutting native trees on-site. This policy achieves an absurdly pure prohibition against minimal cutting of a rapidly renewed resource, at the expense of the visitor's sense of a more natural setting.

The clash of values here is obvious: Without some degree of management, "wildness" cannot survive the number of people who seek to enjoy it. But with too much management, or the wrong kind, we can destroy the spiritual component of wildness in our zeal to preserve its physical side. Often the values we've cited are not in conflict: that is, some steps protect both the resource and preserve the spirit of wildness as well. That the two values can conflict, however, is the point we are seeking to make here.

What Are We Teaching?

The Withitte School's Outdoor Weeks presents us with a clash of other values. Here are almost 100 people tramping through that stretch of the Green Mountains for a two-week period. Each night for 10 nights, 10 fires start up, built (we hope!) from dead and down wood. Then for the last three days, close to 100 individual fires are maintained almost continuously. This is repeated every year in generally the same area.

Our example here is truly fictional, but it draws on a large number of similar educational programs. There is a deep-rooted belief in many educators that the outdoors is a nonpareil laboratory for the development of the human spirit. "Wilderness," "challenge," "adventure" are watchwords of this faith. Thanks to Outward Bound and a host of imitators, along with summer camps, scouting programs, military elite units, supervised gangs from the inner city, progressive secondary schools, and college outing clubs and freshman trips programs, a vigorous faith has gripped a large spectrum of educators that the backcountry provides a unique setting for the most valuable kind of education, a road to self-knowledge, a vehicle for bridging barriers, a special bonding, an uplifting of the spirit. Outdoor trips are, as one New England secondary school leader puts it, "a tonic for tests, a panacea for pressure, a release from reading."

Who can dispute this ardent belief in the powers of wilderness? Not us.

But some people are going to raise questions about the impact on limited forest resources of so many students going into the same forest areas every year, year after year. In our region we learn that certain sections of the mountains are the special targets of this school or that camp or club program or Outward Bound or freshman trips. Walk up a stream valley that has no trail and you suddenly come upon a flattened clearing next to the stream, a network of trampled paths, caved-in banks, woods denuded of down trees, soft woods stripped to a human browse height of all their dry lower branches. Or try to find solitude in that part of the Green Mountains when Withitte's Outdoor Weeks is in progress. These outdoor educators say they are constantly looking for a blank spot on the map to introduce the kids to for a few days. What happens to the blankness of such spots? They are filled in, stamped on, stamped out, indelibly.

Indeed, is anyone here getting a *wilderness* experience? In 90 percent of these programs, definitely not. The woods are being used as a radically different setting and to present unfamiliar challenges. But this is clearly not a wilderness experience. Even the much-trumpeted "solo" is set up under such careful safeguards against any genuine risk that most of the really valuable lessons of solitary adventure are muted beyond recognition.

We are not educators, and are not qualified to pass judgment on the value of these experiences to the participants...but we wonder. We don't share the faith that a one-shot synthetic backcountry experience will forever cure, or even much ameliorate, the problems of adolescence, or of rich boarding-school kids, or of ghetto dwellers, or of nervous college freshmen.

But the point is not so much whether there is value in these programs as whether, on the scale they are currently on and the scale to which they appear to be headed, the backcountry can endure their presence without jeopardy to other values.

Backcountry Comforts: A Contradiction in Terms?

As for that fly-in to Grandview Lodge, provision of full-service facilities in the backcountry certainly does make it easier for those privileged to stay at such places. Who really enjoys carrying food and equipment on their backs, if someone else will supply them?

If you challenge that reasoning, you can quickly look like a masochist or sadist. But in truth, the backcountry experience is not normally a bed of roses. With the very rare exception of those few full-service facilities—in this country almost entirely limited to New Hampshire—everyone expects and has always expected to be self-reliant, to carry all of his or her own needs in and out of the backcountry. The argument that this limits who can enjoy the backcountry is unanswerable. Of course. No one gets to enjoy Sanskrit poetry unless he or she is well educated and takes the trouble to master Sanskrit. No one can enjoy playing string quartets unless he or she is musical and practices. Lots of things in this world are unevenly available. If we set out to make the backcountry equally available to everyone, the resulting backcountry is going to be a very different place from what it has always been.

Certainly the case for making the backcountry available on a broad nondiscriminatory basis falls flat on its face if the resulting full-service facilities then cost more than 100 clams per couple per night. Providing full service at significantly lower cost would be a difficult assignment, but if the theory is to make the backcountry more equally available, the cost needs some working on.

In fact, debate over whether backcountry facilities like Grandview Lodge should exist or not is really a kind of red herring seducing the debate away from the real issue. Grandview Lodge or places like it do exist, and they are not likely to go away in our lifetimes. The real question is, What kind of experience is provided there? A quiet, peaceful evening and morning suited to contemplating the serenity and natural values of the backcountry? Or a crowded, noisy (very noisy: you can't converse at dinner without virtually shouting), sociable, and frightfully expensive experience—all adjectives that clash with many people's concept of the backcountry? Do such facilities put people in touch with wildness? Or do they insulate the guests from wildness? Evening at Grandview Lodge, for most guests, is passed indoors, bright propane lights shutting out the dark of nature's night, the buzz of human noise obliterating the sounds of wind and water, the night's still hours passed in noisy, sociable pursuits like card games and group conversations, almost everyone oblivious to the world of wild nature out there during the night hours, a world that is palpable to campers in a tent or open-front lean-to.

Indeed, perhaps the saddest consequence of overdeveloped, overpriced facilities is that they drive a wedge between the haves and have-nots of the backcountry, creating two distinct populations among hikers, with those on the outside deeply resenting this inappropriate intrusion on the backcountry scene.

The clash of values becomes more apparent when one considers the question of whether concentrating overnight visitors in one large facility may reduce their impact on the forest. That's a legitimate point on which evaluations may differ. Take 50 people and disperse them in tenting groups of two or four; would they disturb the forest habitat more or less than the same 50 concentrated inside one building? Much would depend on the camping style of the 50 tenters. We can get hung up on deploring the modest impact of a few tents and forget that, for many, the presence of a very large building functioning as a high-priced hotel in the heart of the backcountry does a screaming violence to many people's concept of what the very essence of backcountry is all about.

Now about that helicopter. It's a spectacularly efficient way to get supplies in and out, no question. But the presence of an extremely noisy symbol of modern technology droning slowly in and out of the backcountry raises other questions. We have more to say about aircraft in a later chapter, so we'll pass over this one now.

Security versus the Freedom of the Hills

As for Wonder State Park, we propose here to drop the anonymity of our made-up names. In case anyone didn't know, we're talking about Baxter State Park, the management authority in charge of about 200,000 acres surrounding Maine's mightiest mountain, Katahdin.

Baxter Park is supervised by an able and dedicated corps of rangers who believe that safety is a paramount concern in terrain so rugged as Katahdin. They have instituted that long list of procedures that we cited, designed to ensure that no visitor will get hurt. The cause of safety is well served.

But what is the result for visitors? Some seem not to mind, and they are fortunate. For others? "It feels like you're visiting a prison," wrote one hiker. "I wish there were a way to relax these rules and signs that say 'NO....' and still preserve the environs and visitor experience." Paul Petzoldt, the founder of the National Outdoor Leadership School (NOLS), said of his one trip to Katahdin: "It was like a prison camp to me." We know lots of New England outdoorspeople—ourselves included—who never get to visit that magnificent landscape of Katahdin because they do not wish to put up with the essentially insulting game of being watched over day and night.

Baxter Park's apologists sometimes defend these policies by pointing out that they are required to observe the strictures laid down in the deeds under which Percival Baxter donated the land to the state of Maine. These deeds have a lot to say about preserving the land in its natural state, but nothing about going overboard on safety. Preserving the land is irrelevant to such rules as prohibiting hiking in bad weather, starting and stopping times, age limits, and approval of equipment. Preserving the land and spirit of wildness is violated by overblazing and excessive patrol. These policies are focused on safety to the exclusion of other values.

Baxter Park management would do well to heed such messages as Roderick Nash's words:

> The quality of freedom so frequently associated with wilderness is diminished, if not destroyed, by regulation. Campgrounds become sleeping-bag motels with defined capacities and checkout times.... Wilderness, in the final analysis, is a state of mind.... Simply to know that one visits a wilderness by the grace of and under conditions established by government agencies could break the spell for many people.

Values in conflict: perhaps we've sounded our own biases too much in the foregoing discussion. At this point, we're not trying to sell you on any particular hierarchy of values, but simply to underscore the point that equally desirable goals may clash. It is not enough to establish that this or that backcountry activity is desirable. It is mandatory also to evaluate the effect of that activity on the whole spectrum of backcountry values. Highly desirable goals may have a cost. An exhibit cosponsored by the New Hampshire Historical Society and the Society for Protection of New Hampshire Forests in April 1992 was entitled "At What Cost: Shaping the Land We Call New Hampshire." That's a title weighty with meaning. As backcountry managers and as outdoorspeople, in our attitudes toward backcountry we must recognize this concept of cost. Highly desirable goals may have a cost, which perhaps we should not tolerate, in adverse impact on other, extremely important, and sometimes extremely fragile or vulnerable values. And one of the values most at issue and most vulnerable is what this book aims to focus on: the spirit of wildness.

In George Eliot's incomparable novel of humanity *Middlemarch*, Dorothea says: "And I will learn what everything costs." It is one of Eliot's finer lines. Learning what everything costs is what we must do in looking at conflicting values in the backcountry.

6

Why the Lorax Lost

If there is to be a minimum chance of success, there is
only one way to strive for decency, reason, responsibility,
sincerity, civility, and tolerance: and that is decently,
reasonably, responsibly, sincerely, civilly, and tolerantly.

VACLAV HAVEL, *NEW YORK REVIEW OF BOOKS*,
APRIL 9, 1992

LOGGING COMPANIES in the Northwest have protested little
children reading Dr. Seuss's *The Lorax* in public schools. Sinister
propaganda has been detected among the singsong make-believe
doggerel of that modern-day Chaucer of children's literature.

The loggers know the enemy well. *The Lorax* is indeed a
threat to their way of life, if the latter be defined as a relentless
exploitation of limited resources in pursuit of nonsustainable
markets.

If you do not know this particular gem of Seussiana, you
should. Get it; read it; take heed.

But when you do, pay close attention. There is more in *The
Lorax* than either its more ardent fans or its vociferous critics have
noticed, we suspect. It is, the logging censors notwithstanding,

definitely not a one-sided view of reality. Dr. Seuss has a sermon for the conservationist as well as for the exploiters.

Consider, for example: Who wins? Well, nobody really, and certainly not the Lorax. And as in any good Greek or Shakespearean tragedy, it's his own fault. That makes it no less tragedy; indeed, is it not an essential element of high tragedy that Lear, Othello, Oedipus, and Antigone bring on their own fate? So too does the tragicomic figure of the Lorax, in a way. But that only makes the story more realistic, and sad, and relevant to all of us.

Those of our readers who have not read *The Lorax* should be aware that no prose synopsis here can do justice to Dr. Seuss's inspired nonsense-sense. Nor should you miss the illustrations. So be sure to get a copy of the original, then come back and read this chapter again. Meanwhile, we'll try to keep you with us for now.

The obvious villain of the piece is the Once-ler, who destroys the beautiful forest of Truffala trees to supply a fast-growth market of Thneeds, a trivial product that people buy in large quantities until the last Truffala tree is cut. In the process of exploiting the forest of Truffala trees, the Once-ler destroys the habitat for the forest creatures and pollutes the waters therein. The raw material depleted, the market collapses, and the Once-ler is left to live in a depressed area.

You can easily see that the Once-ler and his one-shot exploitative methods are the target of Dr. Seuss. These Northwest loggers sure saw it that way. In truth, the poem is a searing indictment of cut-and-run logging, of the heedless pollution of waters, of the destruction of wildlife habitat, and of the failure to think about the future and to understand the conditions for continued economic development. Dr. Seuss exposes the fallacy of biggering; the horrors of Gluppity-Glupp, also Schloppity-Schlopp; the environmental impact on Brown Bar-be-loots, Swomee Swans, and Humming-fish; and the ultimate disaster resulting from one-shot exploitation and the depletion of this earth's truffalian natural heritage.

But look at some of the other targets that Dr. Seuss's nonsense strikes. Who buys Thneeds? The Lorax perceives little marginal utility for this product, and consequently projects poor sales. But the Once-ler has done his market research. When the first customer comes along, he "happily" buys the first Thneed (at $3.98), and from then on Thneeds are a growth industry.

The entire chain of tragic consequences unleashed by the Once-ler and his production methods would never have occurred had not a sizable proportion of the public "happily" accepted Thneeds as a part of their way of life. There could be no Once-ler without a thoughtless public that adopted Thneeds as a necessity of modern living. Or, better yet, the Once-ler would have sought to produce something else, perhaps something that left undisturbed the Truffala trees and their associated water and wildlife. In the economist George Stigler's felicitous phrase, blaming the producers of frivolous products for the squandering of resources is like blaming waiters for obesity.

Are the eager fans of the Lorax listening? Is it the producers who predestine the destruction of the Truffala forest? Or is it the consumers who demand the products, which producers then eagerly rush to supply? Consumers: that's us, not them.

If we—all of us, not just a few "greedy" corporation executives—did not demand a high volume of petroleum products, for example, the oil companies would not have a market to inspire their relentless search for oil. Please note that many of the modern fabrics and other gear that outdoorspeople buy in preference to wool are derived from petroleum. Furthermore, do we have to buy the new version year after year?

We should not ask our readers to adopt our personal spartan buying habits. We both have a bit of Scottish blood in our veins, which we consistently exaggerate, and you know what a Scotsman does with his old razor blades? (He shaves with them.) So we don't expect everyone to be as frugal (five-dollar word for "cheap") as us. But let us tell you about our windpants.

We had some windpants that had been discarded by two previous owners on the grounds that they were too old, worn, and obsolete. Those windpants became ours in time for the winter season of 1971. They consisted of one piece of ripstop nylon and three elastics. Period. No fly opening, no side vents, no Velcro closures, no zippers, no Gore-Tex, none of a dozen other new special features that make it necessary to discard last year's model for the latest. We wore those windpants from 1971 until 1991, through a lot more winter climbing than most people have time for each winter. The interesting point is that when they finally wore out, the market did not offer any windpants so simple. If we had had the money, we'd have had to buy windpants with half a dozen features we didn't need or want, for a price that amazed us, who had not looked at windpants prices since 1971. Fortunately, a kind seamstress-hiker friend duplicated the old pair with fresh materials (this time in a softer color, but that's another issue). So now we're set for windpants for the next 20 years.

As with windpants, so with countless other items of outdoor gear. As a group, aren't we outdoor recreationists "happily" buying too many Thneeds too often? Aren't we supporting a segment of the petroleum industry that, though small, is bigger than it ought to be?

Another classic children's storyteller, George MacDonald, told his little listeners a message their parents might heed: "To have what we want is riches, but to be able to do without is power."

Doubtless you could catch us with frivolous gear among our paraphernalia. We do not dress exclusively in miff-muffered moof.

What we are saying is that we all should remember: somewhere a Once-ler is cutting a Truffala tree to supply us with these Thneeds. Don't blame the Once-ler. Look in the mirror. No, wait! Don't buy a mirror! Look in the next clear pool of water you come across.

Take another example. The loggers would not be out there cutting spotted owl habitat if we were not all out here demanding forest products, from planed lumber to wood furniture and houses, to the paper that we consume in absurdly wasteful quantities to feed into and out of computers or to produce books that writers like Dr. Seuss and Laura and Guy Waterman feel compelled to write. (We observe that the best-selling books of Dr. Seuss consume a lot more paper than ours.)

Yes, the large corporations do what they can to promote sales through advertising and other marketing tactics. But no one says we, the public, have to go along. It is a point of dispute just how much advertising can create a demand, as opposed to simply tapping into a latent one. You have to have a lot more faith in the power of advertising than we do, and a lot less confidence in the inherent good sense of people, to believe that advertising controls consumer choice that much. It is a dismal view of the public to say that we do not have the intelligence and the good conscience to adjust our consumption patterns to what are, in the long-term, the best interests of the human community and the biosphere on which it rests.

We shall get nowhere in this troubled world as long as we blame our troubles on the tiny minority of corporation executives, whose control over markets is grossly exaggerated, instead of recognizing the responsibility of the entire community to shape its consumption patterns in more environmentally responsible ways. This is one error that the Lorax makes, and so do a lot of the rest of us.

It may seem politically difficult to discipline the thinking and consequent consumption habits of an entire population. Certainly the oil industry doesn't sink or swim on the tiny outdoor-gear segment of its enormous markets.

But strike closer to home—as Dr. Seuss relentlessly does. Those who perceive the problem and are roused to do something about it bear a special responsibility. They are the ones who can rouse public consciousness, initiate the needed dialogue, and argue in the public debate for a more rational policy in the long-term, balanced best interests of all concerned. It is they who can speak for the trees.

In Dr. Seuss's morality play, the Lorax represents that voice. The Lorax is aroused, eloquent, fearless, on the job. But he loses. Why?

Sure, part of the blame rests properly with the Once-ler. We certainly should not let the producers or the corporation executives entirely off the hook. We have to reach them with the message. But that is just what the Lorax signally fails to do. Is it not part of the Lorax's responsibility to find out how to reach them? Is it enough to confront the Once-ler, to shout at him, to marshal the evidence, to predict consequences? To judge by the results, it is not enough. The Lorax loses.

Look at his tactics. When he first appears, he is described as shortish, oldish, brownish, and mossy, with a voice that is sharpish and bossy. He presents facts to the Once-ler, he shows him the consequences of his production methods. But he *is* bossy. He is shrill, angry, and unconcerned with the Once-ler's objectives or viewpoint. He does not discuss; he issues demands.

One of the most pointed passages in this epic is where the Once-ler, hitherto genial and friendly, albeit unresponsive, finally loses his temper and responds in kind to the Lorax's tirades. He hits close to home when he points out that all the Lorax has said amounts to "Bad! Bad! Bad! Bad!" He rises to assert that he has his rights too on this small planet. If the Lorax expresses eloquence to us conservationists, the Once-ler's aroused cry in this passage surely must appear as eloquence to the loggers, the corporation executives, and—most significant—to the myriads of little people with jobs in the industries of exploitation. With their perspective skewed by self-interest, these folks, these good folks, are going to hear the shrill cries of us conservationists as only "Bad! Bad! Bad! Bad!" and they are going to feel that they too have rights as much or more than Brown Bar-ba-loots or Humming-fish or spotted owls or Alaskan wilderness.

The Lorax loses because he fails to develop an approach that succeeds in reaching either the Once-ler or the Thneed-buying consumers, whose buying decisions support the Once-ler's production operations. At least, even at the height of his fury, the Once-ler has the courtesy to address the Lorax as "Sir," while in his opening words the Lorax tags his opponent contemptuously as "Mister."

What would have worked? We don't know, but we again point out that the Lorax lost, and in losing allowed the once-beautiful forest of Truffala trees to degenerate into a dark, deserted, desolation of Grickle-grass.

If those of us who speak for the trees fail in our real world, we should bear as much of the blame as the consumers of Thneeds and the executives of the Once-ler's operations.

It would be easy to be pessimistic in viewing the prospects. Rain forest is disappearing at a frightening daily rate in Latin America; habitat of the last large land mammals on earth is vanishing in Africa; arctic and antarctic regions are being exploited; and world demand for oil and other limited resources keeps "happily" growing beyond all rationality. These trends are destined to continue unless we learn how to reach both the producers and the consumers with the message. Even a contrite Once-ler can see that "UNLESS someone like you cares a whole awful lot, nothing is going to get better. It's not." UNLESS.

II

RESPECT FOR THE MYSTERY

7

The Numbers Racket:
Large Parties and Wildness

In my own life, the change I feel most and deplore most is
crowding, the sense of a world stuffed to bursting with
people.... Will any quiet uncluttered places be left on
earth? Time-sharing in holiday complexes in Katmandu,
package tours to the Kalahari Desert?

MARTHA GELLHORN, THE VIEW FROM THE GROUND

NOW LET'S GET DOWN to cases. Enough generalizations. Let's talk about some very specific things that are going on that ought to stop.

Silence and Sounds

By way of setting the stage, first consider the *sound* of wildness. Most people think of the attractions of the backcountry in terms of sights: striking mountain vistas, the rolling green carpets of hillsides that flame into orange and red in the fall, lovely waterfalls and cascades, intimate miniatures of moss and fern. But the sounds as well as the sights of the backcountry attract the perceptive visitor. And the principal sound to treasure is that of *silence*.

True silence—not just the avoidance of major distracting noises, but that absolute absence of *any* sounds, Pascal's "eternal silence of these infinite spaces"—is rare even in the backwoods. The soft, sweet sounds of the natural world, principally wind and water, are very often present, not to mention birds, animals, and those articulate observers and commentators, the trees. We'll talk about these in a bit. But for now reflect for a moment on how rare is true, absolute silence.

The city dweller rarely ever hears the sound of silence. Houses and apartments abound in a diversity of sounds that we normally take for granted and scarcely "hear" with our conscious minds: heating systems stopping and starting, clocks ticking, refrigerators ruminating the way refrigerators do, radiators clunking nervously, air conditioning units muttering and occasionally expostulating, outside street noises of traffic, children, doors closing, dogs barking, airplanes passing overhead, somewhere a radio. Offices are noisier yet, and libraries possibly noisiest of all.

One of the frustrations of modern life is the impossibility of escaping noise. Even that highest creation of the Muses, music, has been debased by being droned into our ears perpetually in offices, stores, supermarkets, airplanes, elevators, everywhere. The quietest places in modern society formerly were the anterooms of dentists' offices—so quiet you could hear the soft whine of a drill in the next room, remember?—but even here piped-in, innocuous music is now supplied. Few of us command the position of George Bernard Shaw, who was told at a restaurant that the orchestra would play "anything you like—what would you like them to play, Mr. Shaw?" His reply: "Dominoes."

C. S. Lewis's devilish persona in *The Screwtape Letters*, wrote:

> Noise, the grand dynamism, the audible expression of all that is exultant, ruthless, and virile—noise which alone defends us from silly qualms, depressing scruples, and impossible desires.

We will make the whole universe a noise in the end. We
have already made great strides in this direction as regards the
earth. The melodies and silences of heaven will be shouted
down in the end.

Getting away from civilization's cacophony is one major
reason why people value the backwoods and fly to it as to a sanctuary, "gone far away into the silent land," to borrow Christina
Rossetti's nice phrase.

Back in 1869 the Reverend William Henry Harrison Murray,
writing of a sojourn in the woods of the Adirondacks, observed: "It
is the silence of this wilderness that most impressed me." Ever
since, people have been seeking that silence in the wildlands away
from man's noisy works. We can recall many moments, on still days
when the wind was silent, far enough away from any brook, unnoticed for the moment by birds, when we sat perfectly still to hear
that rarest of sounds, its absence. It is a void, almost as awesome as
being on the rim of some vast, bottomless canyon. There is a
mystery in silence. Into this immensity of soundlessness, you could
drop a whisper and it would seem to float interminably through the
abyss. "Speech is of Time, Silence is of Eternity," wrote Thomas
Carlyle. There is indeed a timelessness, a suspension of events in
true silence.

The New York chapter of the Appalachian Mountain Club
once regularly scheduled a unique kind of excursion, known as
"silent walks." They were hikes whose itinerary might be like that
of any other hike, but during which the group periodically walked
for 20 minutes without anyone saying a word. It may sound goofy: a
dozen or more people lumping along the trail without speaking to
one another. Those who have been along, though, say that once
you grow accustomed to it, your eyes open wider to the world
around you, you tune in to the wind and water, and to the sounds
of the woods, and a sense of oneness both within the group and
within the natural world as a whole is felt. We prefer our silence in
smaller numbers, but the idea sounds intriguing.

Backwoods Sounds

Silence, though, is but one of the fascinating sounds of the backwoods. Keats wrote:

> And then there crept
> A little noiseless noise among the leaves,
> Born of the very sigh that silence heaves.

There is the sound of wind, ranging from the sparse rustle of blowing leaves to the shriek of the winter gale above treeline.

There is the sound of water, ranging from the full-throated waterfalls to Coleridge's

> hidden brook
> In the leafy month of June,
> That to the sleeping woods all night
> Singeth a quiet tune.

There are the sounds of birds, ranging through dozens of species. Our favorites for the mountain areas and the backwoods are the chickadee's sociable chatter, the clear and haunting whistle of the white-throated sparrow, the ethereal elusive melody of the thrush, the intricate trills and grace-notes of the tiny winter wren, and the ominous hoarse croak of the huge raven. In his book, *The Lives of a Cell*, Lewis Thomas writes of birdsong: "Behind the glossaries of warning calls, alarms, mating messages, pronouncements of territory, calls for recruitment, and demands for dispersal, there is redundant, elegant sound that is unaccountable as part of the working day."

Dr. Thomas points out how universal is the need for living things to communicate with sound:

> Almost anything that an animal can employ to make a sound is put to use. Drumming, created by the feet, is used by prairie hens, rabbits, and mice; the head is banged by woodpeckers.... Fish make sounds by clicking their teeth, or, like rattlesnakes, get sounds from externally placed structures. Turtles, alligators, crocodiles, and even snakes make various more or less

vocal sounds.... Even earthworms make sounds. Toads sing to each other, and their friends sing back in antiphony.

And frogs. They can fill the night air with their chorus. Christopher Morley has observed of his neighboring frogs:

> This pond is a kind of Union League Club for frogs.... all night long you can hear them reclining in their arm-chairs of congenial mud and uttering their opinions, which vary very little from generation to generation. Most of these frogs are Republican, we feel sure, but we love them no less.

Trees, those rooted monarchs of the forest, are not always silent watchers. The wind plays upon them as unseen hands upon a harp. In a cold snap, when the mercury dips below zero, the trees will crack and snap nearly as loudly as a pistol. Squeaking trees, limb rubbing on limb, can be mistaken for a bird or human voice. Woodsman Roger Chase, a man with a twinkle in his eye, was a ranger at Maine's Baxter State Park. A deft man with a jackknife, he carved a "tree squeak" out of cedar; for, certainly, every woods walker has surely seen—or nearly seen—the elusive "tree squeak."

Not all sounds of nature are welcomed. Two that we could do without, for example, are that penetrating, insistent whine of the mosquito, and the dreadful low dull crack with which a snow slope announces the commencement of a windslab avalanche, with all its destructive fury. These are quibbles, though.

Breaking the Spell

Now, let's pose a situation and consider its implications. We walked over the Tripyramids once, a trio of spiny, pointy little peaks not far from Professor Fay's Passaconaway. It was an unusually windless day. When we were sitting on the middle of the three summits, looking out over the great green vista below we suddenly heard...nothing! No drone of traffic, no chainsaw buzz, no far-off shouts. But also no wisp of wind, no trill of water, no bird chirp. No red squirrel scolding or running through undergrowth. Clouds tiptoed by silently, trees refrained from discussion, rocks eyed us impassively. We sat very still so as to take in this unusual sound.

And then we heard…the ticking, way down in a clandestine pocket, of a small pocket alarm clock that we used to take on camping trips. Just a very small tick, tick, tick, tick, tick. Unpardonable intrusion! We immediately got up to banish the offender, this representative of Swiss cultural heritage, of fine workmanship, of Heidi and William Tell, of humanity's noblest attainments. We took this little artifact of western civilization down the trail to a rock a good distance away, then returned to soak in some more pure silence. And with the silence came a closer communion with the mountain's inner nature. The wildness of the wilderness.

Consider for a moment this question: what single thing could have broken that magic spell fastest (now that we had removed the darn clock)?

You could list several prime candidates: the arrival of a helicopter, or the sound of a radio, for example. But surely one of the quickest and deadliest ways to change that scene, to break that spell, to exorcize the precious spirit of wildness, is the unexpected arrival of a group of 25 hikers. If one or two or three like-minded souls suddenly walk up (or down) the trail, you may find their company congenial, or at least inoffensive, the scene not greatly changed, a fine sense of wildness now shared, and still undiluted. But not even the best-behaved group of 25 is going to do anything less than violence to the spirit of wildness. Even as few as 10. They're apt to be noisier, less observant, more in tune with the easy pleasures of social interaction than with the subtler pleasures of interacting with the world of nature.

We've noticed it with our own friends and ourselves. Neither we nor most of our friends are loud obnoxious types; that's just not our style. Yet when a group of, say, nine of us gets together to do trail work, we can't help noticing that at night, where we've camped, we're just a little more exuberant, a little more playful—in other words, just plain noisier—than we would be if we were in three separate groups of three. Sometimes we notice ruefully that perhaps other nearby campers are not appreciating our high spirits. It's the nature of groups.

Remember Edward Abbey's analogy of the cathedral? Television's Tom Brokaw, a sensitive conservationist, has referred to large groups in the backcountry as "crowding the cathedral." With reference to one lovely western park, Brokaw comments:

> It is a cathedral, that valley, and we cannot worship in its beauty if it is standing room only.

Limiting Group Size

Fortunately, major factions in the backcountry community have recognized that the numbers racket has a significant adverse impact on the backcountry experience. As a result, nearly every responsible hiking club and many backcountry management authorities have embraced voluntary limits.

In our area, for example, New England and New York, most of the major groups call for a limit of 10 to parties in the backcountry. The Green Mountain Club, in its guide to the Long Trail, counsels: "Ten should be considered a maximum group size (including leaders), and 4 to 6 is far better." In the Adirondacks any group of 10 or more must obtain a special permit before camping on state land; a policy designed, according to the Adirondack Mountain Club, "to encourage groups to split into smaller parties more in keeping with the natural environment." In a survey of Baxter State Park visitors up in Maine, 75 percent felt that group size should be limited. In the Catskills, the state agency dispatched a letter to trail clubs asking them to limit group size, especially for off-trail travel, where they urged a limit of six per party. The White Mountain National Forest advises: "Three to four is a good number, but have no more than eight to ten in your group." The Appalachian Trail Conference has requested that parties traveling more than one day on the historic AT keep their size down to 10 or fewer.

The precise number is not important. But it is quite clear that four is fine, more than 10 definitely not OK. In between those numbers, the effect is going to vary according to the sensitiveness of the group and its leader and the nature of the terrain. That large groups are bad news for the backcountry seems to be a general consensus.

Unfortunately, the vote is not quite unanimous. A discouraging number of camp groups and school outings insist on indulging themselves in mass invasion of the woods. Some of these groups make an effort to be considerate of others; some do not seem to notice. Recently we enjoyed a three-day backpack on Vermont's Mount Mansfield. On the first day we saw few people and shared our shelter with just two other individual hikers that night. After a quiet day exploring Mansfield's fascinating nooks and crannies, we returned to find a school group of 22 at the shelter. Well, it was a different experience that night, but we credit that particular school group with remarkably good manners and a genuine effort by the leaders to see that their students both appreciated the natural world and respected the rights of other parties. As we hiked down on the third morning, there came one of those endless trains of school-age hikers. We stopped counting somewhere upward of 50. It was clear the group was poorly led, if led at all, and that both the woods and any other hikers therein were going to have a bad time of it.

Limiting group size is not easy for many camps and schools. Often they have few experienced leaders. Still, the more responsible camps are recognizing that group size is no small consideration. Where they need to send out 20 or more voluble campers with, say, three adult leaders or counselors, now they may break them up into three groups, go to different places, and thus provide much more of a mountain experience for each smaller group, as well as less of a burden on others.

In those parks that lie close to the major megalopolises of the country, the sheer numbers of hikers are such that groups are almost inevitably large.

Take New York State's Harriman Park, scarcely 50 miles from Manhattan. There's a whole lot of hikers in Manhattan and adjacent boroughs. At times there have been as many as 75 differ-ent hiking clubs emanating from New York City. Many of these have traditionally welcomed one and all, and gone traipsing through Harriman Park with 50 or 75 or even 100 hikers in one party. It seems possibly hard-hearted and certainly unrealistic to suggest a limit of 10 for every group in Harriman Park. A problem arises when such groups head elsewhere, however, sometimes to little-used hiking locales, where the environment may be delicate and vulnerable to the impact of foot traffic.

Fortunately, a progressive and concerned president of the New York–New Jersey Trail Conference, Hugh Neil Zimmerman, has led a chorus of responsible voices asking New York–area clubs to be sensitive to the problems of group size. "Limits to protect fragile areas," warns Zimmerman, "are necessary and prudent." Can the tradition of large parties in New York's nearby hills be ac-cepted? Can the old clubs learn new ways to protect the experience of hiking in New York's highly prized nearby hills? Zimmerman argues for a rule of 10 per party:

> Most will welcome the protection effort and understand the need; those who don't, need the education the rule will provide. Club Hike Chairs can and should take the lead by refusing to list imprudent open-meeting hikes...within supporting guidelines set by the club's leaders.
>
> A little self-regulation will go a long way toward preventing restrictions being forced upon the hiking community by properly concerned land managers.

Further north, in New England, the hills are quieter, more vulnerable to group impact, more appropriate places to take special care to preserve the spirit of wildness.

Unfortunately, even here the vote is not unanimous. We have mentioned the voluntary restraints adopted by the Adirondack Mountain Club, Green Mountain Club, Appalachian Trail Conference and others. Alone of the major north country hiking clubs, the Appalachian Mountain Club has declined to place limits on group size. In fact, it sometimes seems as if the

AMC encourages large groups. More and more "Range Walks" by parties of 25 or 30 happy, noisy hikers are scheduled. The club has taken to sponsoring "Development" hikes as a vehicle for fund-raising, with as many well-heeled participants as they can persuade to go. At AMC's backcountry huts, large groups are given prefer-ence over smaller parties. As hotel managers, perhaps AMC likes to see those big bloc bookings, with all that revenue assured. That's understandable. But backcountry facilities are not commercial hotels, and the AMC surely doesn't want to see them run that way. Sooner or later the club will undoubtedly come around to giving greater weight to the impact of large groups on other guests at the huts, not to mention every hiker passed on the trail, on the quiet mountaintop, along the still shore of each pond. We'd like to hope such consideration will eventually be shown. But during the 1980s, at a time when the other major clubs initiated limits on group size, the AMC expanded the sponsorship of large parties, flouting the request of the White Mountain National Forest managers through whose forest they pass, the Appalachian Trail managers whose trail they tread, and the concerns of every other individual trying to enjoy a little of the spirit of wildness in these hills.

Education and Group Size: What Message?

Some relate this issue of group size to what is really an altogether different issue: should we encourage more people to experience the mountains or not? That is an interesting question on which opinions may legitimately differ. But even if you fervently believe that the future of the mountains depends on encouraging a lot of people to experience them firsthand, it is still far better that such experiences be in small groups.

If your goal is to educate people in the mountains, you know that education is far more effective in smaller groups than large. That's why colleges like to boast (where they can) of their rela-tively small student-to-teacher ratios. What is true in the classroom is even more true in the outdoors: the smaller the group, the more effective the education. On a mountain you can't educate very much if your group is straggling along a quarter mile of trail or (oh no!) spread out over an acre of alpine tundra.

We taught for 14 years at a winter mountaineering school and knew well that when we had a party of six or eight, we could teach. When we had a party of 17 it was a scramble to keep from losing anybody or having them lapse hypothermic unnoticed. That wasn't education, it was just survival.

So no matter how strongly you may believe in introducing a healthy political majority to the joys of the backcountry, for their sakes, and the mountains', and other hikers', do so in small groups.

It is a question of values. What is the essential quality of the backcountry experience that we are trying to preserve? It can be fun to be in a large crowd of garrulous friends, as at a cocktail party. But should we export cocktail party values to the backcountry?

The British climber C. H. Herford wrote a poem called "On Stillness" in which he evoked the message that the quiet of highcountry sounds:

> To whom the mountain stillness is a song
> More sweet and strong
> Than all by human art and rapture poured
> From voice or chord.

The caring steward of the backcountry will want to leave the mountain stillness, that serenity of the wild, undisturbed for the benefit of others. Ultimately the traveler who is in sympathy with the woods and hills will want to preserve that serenity not just for himself or herself, and not just for everyone else who may come there, but also for the sake of the woods and hills themselves. Cocktail party values simply offend the land itself. Wilderness is no place for the numbers racket.

8

Exploitation by Any Other Name

The woods are made for the hunters of dreams,
The brooks for the fishers of song.
SAM WALTER FOSS, *THE BLOODLESS SPORTSMAN*

INAPPROPRIATE GROUP SIZE is just one of many ways in
which the spirit of wildness may be violated even without physical
damage. Let's consider some more specifics.

Quiet Colors, Noisy Colors

A very simple example involves the colors of our clothing and gear.
Before World War II most backwoods apparel was about as colorful
as an accounting exam. Our parents wore old clothes of various
browns, tans, drab greens, or grays. The most you saw of red was in
those classic heavy wool red-and-black-checkered lumberman's
shirts and jackets. They were no more exciting than checkers
either, and they weren't supposed to be. Orange was reserved for
football jerseys. You never saw it in the woods. Tents we recall
from childhood in the 1930s and 1940s were wonderful old canvas

things, perennially musty smelling, of a kind of noncolor somewhere between brown, drab, and dirty.

But after World War II, ripstop nylon and other new fabrics
took over the backpacker's world. *Now* you saw some action on
the color front. Flaming scarlets, electric blues, neon greens, and
international orange blew on the scene with blaring trumpets.
When you arrived on the shore of a pristine wilderness lake, there
could be no missing the presence of another party if their orange
tent beamed at you across the waters, or if they were stalking the
shores in raucous red parkas.

During the 1980s Lycra tights swept the technical climber's
world, and the cliffs were ablaze with fantastic skin-tight color
displays. The unmistakable message from such vivid outfits was,
We are not in a wilderness, and I am not in the slightest concerned with fitting into the landscape; this is an outdoor gymnasium, and I am a gymnast trying to direct your attention from the
land to me.

Park managers in Mount Rainier National Park have found
that when "drab colors" are used by tenters they are less visible,
"and more can use the same general area without knowing of
others' presence." The Rainier managers ask people to think
about color: "As more and more seek the solitude of the wilderness, visual impact will become increasingly important."

If the clothing of the earth is normally primitive and basic—
earthy—should we not clothe ourselves and our accessories in like
vein? Don't we want to become more a part of nature's world, not
proclaim our foreignness to it? Parkas and pants of soft greens and
grays might even help our feeling of fitting in better. But regardless of
the effect on ourselves, such hues will certainly do less violence to
the experience of others if we come to the woods less conspicuously.

Perhaps a modest exemption could be allowed during
hunting season. When hikers and hunters are both loose in the
same woods, the former may be well advised *not* to blend in too
well. Certainly don't let your white handkerchief trail outside
your hip pocket, in imitation of a white-tailed deer. But a simple
bright-red cap should be enough to keep from being shot.

The New Exploiters

Conspicuous presence in the backcountry is a common theme of several related offenses that we'd like to consider next. We'll give you five examples. Another common theme of these five examples is a confusion of worthy ends with wholly inappropriate means.

• Plastic tape in the woods seems singularly at odds with the natural world. It is disconcerting, therefore, to note how many excuses seem to have surfaced in the past few years for leaving brightly colored plastic ribbon in the remote backcountry. When cross-country skiers want a trail, they string ribbons of bright plastic tape from trees. When trail crews plan to put in water bars and make other needed repairs, they tie bright plastic tape at each specific site where work will be done—dozens along some trails. When winter climbers in pursuit of 4,000-footers in winter worry that they might not find the trail in deep snow, rather than schooling themselves in the skills of trail finding and joyously responding to the challenge of staying on an obscure trail, they string it all up with bright plastic tape, perhaps so they can return the same way another day. We've found plastic tape in other places where its function was indecipherable. Perhaps some research project? Some management plan?

In our view, plastic ribbon in the backcountry is litter— pure, basic litter of a most unforgivable kind.

Presumably each offender in the above examples has lofty goals. Surely if they thought about the effect of plastic ribbon on the spirit of wildness, they could adjust their means to achieve those ends in a more appropriate way. Take the use of ribbon to mark trail work, for example: the least we could expect is that trail managers mark trail work stations just before the work is to begin. The practice of carelessly allowing a long lead time between putting up ribbons and getting the work done (and taking *down* the ribbons) is something that could occur only when people are getting too casual about wilderness values. Backcountry managers who care enough will see to it that they

plan and schedule their work thoughtfully, so that the ribbon is not
there long.

• Friends of ours reported a recent hike on Vermont's "footpath in the wilderness," the Long Trail, where they came upon
miles and miles of some sort of white thread stretched along the
trail. They kept getting their boots and walking staffs tangled in
the stuff. For a while they tried to pick it up, on grounds that it
constituted litter, but it went on so long that the chore became
tedious. Our friends were at first puzzled whence it came. Some sort
of modern-day Hansel and Gretel stratagem? Would the string
eventually lead to a cottage made of bread and cakes, and window
panes of clear sugar? No, most Long Trail shelters are less tasty
(though some porcupines evidently think otherwise). The long
spool of string turned out to be some well-meaning but definitely
ill-considered experiment by forest managers to measure trail
mileage.

• One winter we took a long walk in a marvelous secluded
valley known as the Bowl, tucked within a curving rim of forested
mountainside in Professor Fay's beloved Sandwich Range. The
good citizens of nearby Wonalancet campaigned very early—
almost a century ago—to have this area protected from logging.
Under the aegis of the White Mountain National Forest, the
loggers have been kept out of the Bowl to this day—but not the
researchers! We had expected to enjoy a virgin forest, with all the
quiet, untrammeled, peaceful spirit that that implies. What did we
find instead? At repeated intervals, we encountered groups of trees
bedecked with brightly colored plastic ribbons (a neon pink at one
spot). At one location an iron pipe had been thrust into the
ground and painted white, to stand there among the virgin trees,
which had been spared from the loggers. At another spot we found
metal tags stuck on various trees, each inscribed with the runes of
modern science.

• On the Franconia Ridge, a magnificent high walk in the
sky, scientists undertook to measure the extent of vegetation at

various points along the ridge. This experiment first was under-
taken during the 1970s, an era when the dominant group in the
rock-climbing community was deciding that responsible ethics on
their part required abstaining from placing bolts in the rock. Yet
at this very time when the climbers were refraining from placing
bolts, the researchers on the ridge pounded bolts squarely into
prominent boulders, where they protruded as a visual blight and,
in a few cases, a tripping hazard, for passing hikers. Then they
proceeded to paint red numbers on the rocks—more of those
runes used by modern researchers. Astonishing! During the very
years when hikers were getting everyone to understand that
graffiti on trees or backcountry shelters was thoroughly inappropriate, offensive, and downright insupportable, here were the
scientists painting their graffiti right on the exposed rocks of this
fine wild alpine ridge.

• One of the wonders of the modern New England hiker's
world is a magnificent map of the Mount Washington Range.
Produced by the Boston Museum of Science, in collaboration
with the Mount Washington Observatory and the Appalachian
Mountain Club, it is a marvel of scientific precision and aesthetic
beauty. Everyone loves it. But…there is a story behind its production that illustrates how good ends, mingled with well-
intentioned means, can spawn unlooked-for side effects.

In 1978 the Mount Washington map was conceived.
Beginning the following summer, the mappers began installing
large metal "targets," painted a brilliant orange, on every summit
in the range. To do so, they hired a helicopter to drone over the
mountains on many occasions, carrying large and incredibly noisy
electric drills, along with a 65-pound gas-powered electric genera-
tor for drilling holes in the rock so as to mount their colorful
targets.

When hikers raised objection to the immediate noise of the
machines, as well as the lasting visual impact and inappropriate-
ness of these targets, the mapmakers listened considerately. They
gave us assurances that the offending markers would be there for

only one summer. Well, the work bogged down, and those inappropriate hunks of metal adorned the peaks of the Presidentials for most of the 1980s. Give the mapmakers credit: they regretted the delays more than anyone did. They heard the critics, and they wanted to remove those markers as soon as possible. But in their minds, the completion of the map came first; the restoration of the natural mountaintop could wait if it had to.

Summit markers were not all. At some measuring points, the scientists put up substantial, if temporary, observation stands. In the woods, for the purpose of precise location of trails, they affixed white markers to numerous trees. For much of their work they employed helicopters to ferry them around—"most pleasurable," said one report.

The mapmakers' feelings about the helicopters illustrate a ramification of the problem. To them the helicopter was a useful tool, possibly even indispensable. Perhaps at first they hoped to limit its use, out of consideration for the quiet mountain environment. But after a while that sort of concern got shoved under the rug. Eventually they began to joke about their helicopter rides, with a tone of insiders enjoying a privilege denied to outsiders:

> When our work on [Mount] Franklin was done, we stretched out in the sunshine right along Crawford Path, to wait to be picked up [by helicopter]. Along came two perspiring hikers, beginning to doubt whether they would make it up Mount Washington. "You guys seen a helicopter around here? We could sure use one!" "No, not lately." "Funny, I could have sworn I heard one." No answer—

In other words, it's OK for us scientists to use the helicopter all we want, but not for the common perspiring hiker. Let them sweat.

The new map, which was issued after 10 years of this effort, is an unexcelled masterpiece. For detailed bushwhacking, it is unbelievably revealing. As a wall hanging—it's not small—it is a thing of beauty and class. As a monument to the mapmakers, it's a well-earned memorial. But...at what cost to the mountain spirit, over how many years?

Again: A Question of Values

These examples we've cited—from blaring bright parkas to voluble parties of 25 to scientists and mapmakers mucking up the woods—what do they have in common? All represent a failure to respect the wildness in wilderness. They treat the mountain world as a personal playground. They exhibit a kind of elitist arrogance: if I'm advancing the cause of recreation or of science or of education or some other laudable objective, then I'm licensed to act as I please in the wilderness, introduce what intrusions suit my personal agenda, and let the spirit of wildness retreat until I'm through.

Despite their lofty aims, these offenders constitute the new exploiters of the backcountry. Fortunately their impact is lighter and less lasting than that of the old exploiters, the cut-and-run loggers and the strip miners. But surely, if these new exploiters claim to have the good of the backcountry at heart, they too will desire to maintain higher standards.

James North, writing in *American Hiker*, has expressed it well:

> The idea of low-impact travel needs to be broadened and redefined. Today, it's largely considered in terms of one's effect on the environment: leaving no trace when you depart the mountains. But that's no longer enough. Hikers should strive to leave no trace while they're in the mountains as well. Low-impact should not be seen just as one's effect on the environment, but also the effect on others who may happen to share the backcountry at any given time.

To that we would add that it is not just the experience of our fellow hikers that is at stake. There is also the integrity of the wilderness sphere itself. Somewhere is there a Lorax who speaks for the trees? Is there a strong latent sentiment for the spirit of wildness that can manifest itself in vigilant protest against intrusions of inappropriate behavior and associated artifacts? Is the preservation of wildness in all its attributes a legitimate and significant aim of public policy and private conduct? This book is written with the fervent hope that these questions may be answered affirmatively.

Case Study

Slouching toward Lake Wietelmann

The darkness drops again; but now I know
That twenty centuries of stony sleep
Were vexed to nightmare by a rocking cradle,
And what rough beast, its hour come round at last,
Slouches toward Bethlehem to be born?

W.B. YEATS, "THE SECOND COMING"

ON MARCH 15, 1979, the two of us were camped at a remote, densely forested site six and a half miles from the nearest road, on a mantle of three or four feet of snow. That morning the temperature read $-11°F$. But it being mid-March, we guessed that the mercury would rise speedily. So we had our simple breakfast of instant oatmeal and hot chocolate in the dark, and by the first steel gray light of dawn we were strapping our snowshoes on with mittened hands. Within a few minutes the vigor of bushwhacking through the snow-laden forest of spruce, fir, and birch warmed us thoroughly. An earlier thaw, rain, and a deep refreeze left the surface of the snow well consolidated, so progress was much more rapid than usual for winter.

Our bushwhack course followed the valley of a winding brook, which led away from the only nearby trail, up between steep mountain sides, and into a large glacial cirque with two or three spacious pockets. Scrutinizing our topographical map and trying to relate that to the snowbound landscape around us, we made a couple of lucky guesses on which stream forks to follow, and by midmorning we suddenly broke over a small rise, through a dense wall of trees, and found ourselves at a tiny mountain pond, perhaps a single acre in extent, almost a perfect circle, rimmed with woods at its shores and nearly enclosed by towering mountainsides rising steeply more than 1,000 feet above.

The position of that pond is such that, almost surrounded by trailless mountain ridges, it is invisible from any hiking trail, save one or two distant open summits. Even from them the nature of the pond is not discernible. It is absolutely one of the loveliest hidden jewels in the White Mountains. On that winter morning its ice surface lay under deep unbroken snow, a pure white gem cast in a rugged setting.

We crossed on snowshoes, our tracks a sacrilege on the purity of that scene, and struck through a small belt of woods to the base of an open landslide scar. This open slide, perhaps 1,000 feet high, was white with well-compacted snow in most places, pale blue with gleaming water ice in patches. Here we exchanged snowshoes for crampons, dug out a second ice-climbing tool from our packs, and clawed up the 1,000-foot slide, reveling in the emerging mountain vistas above that enchanted circle of white pond below our feet. At the top of the slide we changed back to snowshoes, mushed on upward through the denser, low-growing, stunted and twisted forest of that elevation, to reach the barely discernible, unbroken track of a hiking trail up there at 4,500 feet. We followed the trail to a couple of different summits. One of them was a cause of special celebration that day, as one of us completed her second time around the 4,000-footers of New Hampshire in winter. Then, as light began to slant into late afternoon, we struck back to a point we had carefully selected, plunged back into the thick forest, found a suitable route down the steep mountainside into our morning's cirque, managed to find our tracks of the morning, and retraced them back to our tent as the last light faded. It was one of our finest days in the winter hills.

We love to name mountain features we find. It happened that March 15, 1979, was the 60th birthday of Whitey Wietelmann, a wartime shortstop for the Boston Braves, a .215 hitter in his one full season of 1943, but nevertheless the idol of a certain 11-year-old Boston-area resident of that time who now found himself on the shores of this remote mountain pond on Whitey's 60th birthday. An infinitely patient and generous wife, who inexplicably does not happen to care for The National Pastime, assented to the naming of our lovely one-acre pond by what seemed (to her husband) the only logical name, Lake Wietelmann. To the eye of us beholders, the 1,000-foot snow-and-ice slide above Lake Wietelmann was formed in the image of a map of Korea. So it became the Korea Slide.

During several winters of the 1980s our snowshoes returned to snowbound Lake Wietelmann, sometimes accompanied by friends, who invariably responded to the enchanted spot with the same silent awe and delight that had gripped us on Whitey's birthday, 1979. We introduced ice-climbing friends to the challenge of the Korea Slide. That quiet cirque became a spot of special charm for us.

But for some reason we went all through the 1980s without ever visiting that secluded spot in summer. It is entirely possible that we subconsciously feared that the summertime experience would not be so privileged. Perhaps the pond was a slough of mud, largely grown in, with a tawdry stand of cattails and junk weeds. Perhaps its shores would be choked with brambles or hobblebush or that bushwhacking nightmare, low horizontally growing alders. Perhaps it was better to retain only the clean white memory of Lake Wietelmann in its snowy mantle.

Finally, on October 1, 1990 (on the eve of the 39th anniversary of Bobby Thomson's play-off-winning homer, do you remember—oh, never mind, never mind), a group of five of us made the pilgrimage in early autumn. We walked in from the road, covering the six and a half miles of trail in about three hours. Then we began our bushwhack, following the brook bed, sometimes even rock-hopping up the lively brook itself. The rugged mountain walls gradually encircled us, the trail receding in the distance, the sense of isolation rising palpably.

Finally we crested the last rise and thrashed through the last trees. Then we saw it. Our fears were groundless. No muddy slough, no brambles tangle. Lake Wietelmann was if anything even more an autumn jewel than a winter gem. Its waters lay pure and clear, rippled gently by a faint breeze. The shores were a kind of thick waist-high grass, now tawny with the approaching cold, perfectly easy to walk through. Several convenient boulders lined the edge, ideal lunch spots. On the lower scree of the mountainsides, a few vivid colors stood out against the granite—the birch leaves' yellow, the blueberry bushes' crimson, the conifers' deep green. The mountain rims stood stark, high above, against the blue sky. Lake Wietelmann surprised and bewitched us on that day as it had in winter. After an hour of hushed conversation and reflection, we turned to go. At that precise moment, some kind god instructed a white-throated sparrow to sound its summer song, almost never heard in October. (Ornithologists tell us juvenile birds sometimes begin to practice song just before migrating south.) Anyone who knows that clear, mournful sound, the aural symbol of the spirit of mountain wildness, can appreciate the effect it had on those five favored human souls who stood listening on that crystal day on the enchanted shores of Lake Wietelmann.

Now we began our return to civilization. It was a ruder, more sudden awakening than anticipated. One member of our party had read a guidebook describing recommended hikes in the White Mountains, including, we were dismayed to hear, an off-trail visit to this very pond. We did not have that guidebook along—indeed, the two of us have never seen it—but our friend recalled that the guidebook author recommended following a long-abandoned wood road that contours above the north bank of the brook. This part of the forest was logged thoroughly in the 1890s, and such abandoned wood roads are commonly found and followed on bushwhacks. Our friend had mentioned the guidebook's disclosure of this particular road on the way in, but we had chosen to follow our brookside itinerary familiar from the winter visits. On the way out we five agreed to try to find the guidebook's suggested woodroad.

We found it all right. So had a number of others. What we found was a clearly discernible track worn by footsteps through the woods. Not yet a full trail, and not yet continuous, but in many places an unmistakable trough of footsteps. In wet spots the track had been worn to mud. Where slanted, water was starting to erode the bank. What a contrast with the unmarred wilderness way we had followed coming in.

A technical point, you might call it, should be introduced at this stage for the benefit of any readers who are not yet aware of it. When one or two parties a year, maybe a few more, traverse a typical stretch of northeastern mountain forest, they can leave literally no trace of their passing. Our healthy, fast-growing woods easily recover from the few footsteps; mosses and ferns survive and grow back vigorously; dry leaves blow over whatever footprints are made; nature restores itself fully. This is a highly significant point to eastern wilderness. It means that a certain low volume of off-trail traffic can be accommodated with literally zero loss of wilderness qualities. The next party will never know whether someone else has ever passed there before them. The precious illusion of exploration and adventure can be preserved for all who seek it.

But at some volume of use, this process of restoration ceases. At some undetermined but relentlessly existent number of footsteps, the impact remains. The land is scarred.

The authors of a fine little guide to waterfalls of the White Mountains, Bruce and Doreen Bolnick, wisely filled their guide with cautions to the waterfalls seeker to tread with care and concern for the fragile surroundings. The Bolnicks put it well when they warned: "Sometimes 'leaving nothing but footsteps' is leaving too much."

That other guidebook, by describing in print the route to Lake Wietelmann, began to tip the balance in the volume of visitors to its shores. It moved the pond's "use level" (in backcountry managerial jargon) from essentially zero impact to a distinctly discernible adverse one.

We came away from that last trip to Lake Wietelmann with our minds full of thoughts about what we had seen—not only the quiet beauty of the pond but also the early, lasting signs of the destructive presence of humans. The issue we wish to raise now, and to pursue in the following chapter, is the relationship of guidebooks to the spirit of wildness.

9

Guidebooks and Wildness

The very nature of the trail-guide beast cuts clear across
this grain: the "sensible" subordination of doubt and
chance; the mile-by-mile scheduling and checking; the
rule of the written word. It is all inapplicable, stupid. It
walls off, before you have even begun, the values you
came so far to retrieve.

COLIN FLETCHER, *THE COMPLETE WALKER III*

COLIN FLETCHER, the great prophet of pedestrianism, once
vented his fury on guidebooks. Fletcher argued that the purpose of
being in the backcountry was to see it all, to take it all in, not just
to get from trailhead A to peak B or campsite C. He felt strongly
that the hiker saw most who had to plan, scout, and explore his or
her own way. Guidebooks, cried Fletcher, "gnaw at the taproots of
what I judge wilderness walking (or any kind of sane walking) to be
all about."

That may seem a stern and undiluted doctrine, and most
hikers will always choose to compromise by consulting trail guides
for planning itineraries and ensuring against confusion or getting
lost.

But Fletcher's point is worth our attention. For example, when our goal is to explore off-trail, to visit the inner heart of the forest or mountain world, how much explicit direction do we want? Is not a little confusion part of the deal, part of the excitement and adventure?

Let's go back to that experience we told about on the way out from Lake Wietelmann. We complained in the last chapter about the incipient physical degradation that a guidebook description had launched. But that small beginning of physical degradation was only one result. Less obvious but perhaps more critical was the increased foot traffic's impact on the spirit of wildness. Before that muddy track was worn, any visitor to Lake Wietelmann had an almost religious experience, feeling the trail recede below, the mountain walls close in, the stream bubbling its course from some unknown source, to be revealed only by guessing right at several stream junctions and by picking a way upward through a mysterious woods, with a hint of uncertainty right up to the last magic moment. The book-guided visitor has a completely different experience, following a set of directions and looking for obvious signs that others had been this way—no mystery, no demands, no wonder, no uncertainty, and in the end no magic. When in doubt, let's have a look at that book again. How that printed page or two undermines the spirit of wildness!

A strong and benevolent impulse to share motivates many clubs and individuals—including guidebook writers—to advertise access to the hidden places of the backcountry. Sharing is a generous quality. We love to share the wilderness world. What is difficult, but maybe not impossible, is both to share and to preserve.

The key to both sharing and preserving is to think and think hard: *what* are we sharing? Is it just the physical event of standing on the shores of Lake Wietelmann? Is it just some sensory inventory of water, sky, vegetation, mountainside? Is that really all there is to that puddle of water in the wilderness?

If we think about it, we begin to consider, for Lake Wietelmann or any other such hidden, little-visited spot, whether or not the essence of the experience is discovery, the progressive withdrawal from aids like trails and guidebooks, the sense of emerging remoteness. Just a little bit of uncertainty is one key: Did we take the correct fork back there? Should we instead be way over *there*? What will we find when we crest the rise ahead?

We've made our share of blunders off-trail. Maybe we've never been lost in the woods, but we've sure been mightily confused. We know what it is to be, in the sportsman Frank Woolner's fine phrase, "humiliated in the field." But that's what gives spice to the adventure, and joy to success.

On one cold winter day, three of us set out, loaded with rope and ice-climbing gear (heavy!), to find a hidden cascade of ice in the lower end of Crawford Notch, with dreams of making its first ascent. A wrong turn or two, too easy acquiescence in sticking with the easier track of an old wood road, and a generous measure of overconfidence in our sense of direction, and we presently realized that we were rising to a most remarkable elevation for the base of a good-sized waterfall. Eventually we found ourselves on the top of a 3,706-foot mountain. We can reliably report that no waterfalls come to an end on the top of this particular mountain. We solaced ourselves that day with the confident knowledge that we had made the first winter ascent of Mount Bemis with full technical climbing gear (to repeat: heavy!). As far as we know that hidden waterfall remains unclimbed to this day.

A disappointment? Of course. But without such occasional humiliations, the prize of success would have less worth.

Getting to Lake Wietelmann is nothing. *How* you get there is everything. There are other beautiful places to which trails and guidebooks lead, and they may be enjoyed with relatively modest effort. Should there not also be places that require something more of the visitor, something much more; and by requiring more, give more as well?

More and more people are asking what are the proper limits for guidebooks. At a 1991 Banff Festival of Mountain Films a panel of three authors debated the issue of whether a guidebook creates the demand for access to an area or whether the demand created the book. The title of the panel was "Guidebooks: A Moral Dilemma."

One who is both a writer and a hiker with a keen sensitivity about this dilemma, Peter Crane of the Mount Washington Observatory, has cautioned:

> Writing can be personally satisfying and can help put bread on the table, but we have to recognize that those motives, which in themselves are not ignoble, cannot justify and should not lead us to rationalize giving unneeded publicity to socially or ecologically fragile areas.

A brief story about a rock-climbing guidebook illustrates a point here. Back in the 1960s the only guides to rock climbs on the East's biggest cliff, Cannon Mountain, were brief and focused exclusively on Cannon Cliff itself. They did not cover a large number of outlying crags in the same general area. As climbing at Cannon became more popular in the 1970s, one of the leading locals, Howard Peterson, undertook to publish the first full book of Cannon climbs. Initially Peterson planned to expand the scope to include all the cliffs and crags nearby. Then Peterson, after some long thoughtful conversations and correspondence with other climbers, reconsidered. As a result, he concluded that there was real value in leaving the outlying crags undescribed, unpublished, left for adventurous climbers to explore and discover in a spirit wholly different from guidebook climbing.

When Peterson's guidebook appeared in 1975, he wrote this preface, reprinted here in its entirety:

> Though there are many crags in the Franconia Notch area, this guide will only give route descriptions to Cannon Cliff, a cliff where route ascents have been documented for 40 years. I would like to thank those who have urged that additional crags be excluded, leaving their continual discovery to those pursuing the freedom of the hills. It is hoped that all will respect this direction.

When you read those deceptively simple three sentences, you can appreciate their author's self-restraint (uncommon in guidebook writers), humility, sensitivity to wilderness qualities, fine sense of

values, and ability to strike a nice balance between, on the one
hand, sharing the pleasures of backcountry recreation (Peterson
does describe all the climbs available at the time on Cannon Cliff)
and, on the other, respecting the different but equally valid pleasures of a quieter and more personal exploration. Where, oh where,
are the Howard Petersons among guidebook writers today?

Those who deplore excessively detailed guidebooks want to
share something too. They want to share a spirit of adventure and
self-reliance and mystery and wonder. Do we really share the
hidden jewels of the woods if we publish them to the world? Or do
we, rather, deny the adventurous the opportunity of exploring and
a sense of the wildness? And in the process we worsen, or even
initiate, the physical degradation of that spot. When we raise "use
levels" to the point that footprints and erosion remain indelibly,
don't we destroy much more than we create?

Yes, "use" will be less if there is no guidebook. Fewer absolute
numbers of people will see Lake Wietelmann. In the terms in
which Disney attractions measure success, we'll have fewer results
to show. But maybe that's the fallacy of looking at people as blocs,
as numbers, as aggregates. Look at them as individuals, and within
the masses you'll find a few individuals who will step away from the
crowd and look for the path least traveled, the hidden and more
demanding route.

There is nothing elitist or exclusive about backcountry
adventure in any sense that deserves disapprobation. There are no
bars based on race, creed, or national origin, no educational
requirements, no fraternal password or handshake. Anyone can
find these hidden jewels on their own—with only one stipulation,
only one barrier, and that is that you must decide it's important
enough to you to devote time to learning the ways of the mountain, to mastering the art of reading the map and (much, much
more important than map reading) reading the terrain. You must
want to make the mountains your world.

Anyone can do it. The idea that only fit young males can enjoy
wilderness has been irrefutably squashed for all time by the formation
of a Colorado-based organization called Great Old Broads for Wilder-

ness. With membership limited to women over 45, GOBW was founded, according to one leader: "on the proposition that everyone is, or will be, or would like to be a woman 45 years of age or older." The members rock climb, ice climb, mountaineer, and generally explore wilderness areas of the West. Though their name is inspired by their obvious delight in fun and good times, GOBW also actively and seriously lobbies for protection of wilderness, an irrefutable case that wilderness is for everyone who cares.

There are no arcane disciplines required for appreciation of wild country, no aptitude for mathematics or foreign languages, nothing that makes a prerequisite of social standing or a middle-class upbringing. It is a very egalitarian world up there in the hills. The mountain gods never look at your academic credentials or birthright. But they do inspect rigorously your qualifications in the arts of finding your way in the mountains.

Maybe this has to do with the difference between democracy and mobocracy. The wilderness is truly democratic, no respecter of persons, but it is not for the mob. Maybe this is Thomas Jefferson's idea of natural aristocracy, as applied to wilderness, and Jefferson was a true democrat (or, to use Dwight Eisenhower's phrase from a different context and lowering his uppercase D, a discerning democrat).

There are two things we are trying to save, two things we are trying to share. One is the physical integrity of the place and the way to it. The other is the spirit of wildness and the spiritual joys of adventure, mystery, difficulty, and wonder. Roger Angell, a perceptive observer of other scenes than wilderness, has warned:

> We want to make an exhibition out of everything, we want everything to be immediately accessible, but some things are better left to memory and imagination.

Case Study

The Future of Melville Cascades

He went through the Wet Wild Woods, waving his wild tail, and walking by his wild lone. But he never told anybody.

RUDYARD KIPLING,
"THE CAT THAT WALKED BY HIMSELF,"
JUST SO STORIES

THERE ONCE WAS a trail to Melville Cascades. But trails in that area took a terrible beating from the 1938 hurricane, and many were never restored. War followed, interrupting trail work. Hiking patterns changed after the war, and some trails simply were abandoned for good. In our New England climate, it didn't take long for the forest to grow over a footpath that never had seen heavy traffic in the manner of later years like the 1970s. Soon the trail to Melville Cascades was gone.

Our little party in the 1980s saw almost no trace of the ancient track. We bushwhacked through the twisted tangle of

conifers, comfortable and familiar in their prickly, grasping closeness. Much of the time we rock-hopped along the stream that
drains the cascades, finding a long series of lovely rills and pools.

What held us spellbound, though, was what lay along the
stream's edge: a flooring of spagnum moss so thick, so soft that an
occasional footstep nearly submerged a boot. How luxuriant, how
vibrantly, intensely green! A carpet fit for emerald princesses.

Suddenly we were at the falls, and conversation ceased as we
paused to contemplate that watery rush. Yes, Melville Cascades
certainly is one of the most beautiful in Vermont. But it is something more, as a glance at the sides of the falls showed.

Everyone knows what the ground alongside a roadside or
trailside waterfall looks like. Go to Kent State Falls in Connecticut, or Kaaterskill Falls in the Catskills, or even walk up about a
mile to Cloudland Falls in Franconia Notch, or into Arethusa Falls
in Crawford Notch, both in New Hampshire. These are beautiful
falls, and it is wonderful for everyone to have access to spectacular,
refreshing, enchanting bursts of water like them. But wild they are
not: The ground around them is rammed-earth hardpan, devoid of
ferns or moss, evergreen roots exposed, the dark packed earth
becoming a slippery mud bank in every rain, wherein it further
erodes in slimy smears. That is the price of access. It's well worth
paying to give large numbers of people unrestricted entry to such
displays of natural beauty.

But now go back mentally to Melville Cascades. What does
the ground around it look like? See, mentally, that lush spread of
hanging mosses and lichens and ferns, that verdant understory.
That mosaic of rich and varied green, soft and springy, remains wet
long after rains. It is terribly vulnerable and entirely defenseless.
Should a large number of hikers regularly troop around Melville
Cascades, it would be degraded immediately; in a few weeks or
months of high visitor "use" (good term here), that rich, soft, wet,
green cover would be lost.

You may well ask whether we are not impinging upon this
fragile scene simply by going there. The answer is both yes and no.
Yes, our small party is painfully aware of its footprints in the moss

bed, wherever we are forced to take a step there. But no, as long as we are one of a very small number that come and go, that impact should not last. If we are scrupulously careful while we're there— step on rock as much as possible, keep off the steeper and more unstable slopes, try carefully not to kick divots, spread out when we must cross the most fragile areas—then nature will repair our small imprint quickly and just about completely.

The question is, How many of us go to Melville Cascades? And the second question is, How many is too many?

Both questions have some urgency because a proposal has been placed before the responsible land managers to reopen the 1930s trail to Melville Cascades. Opinions within the Green Mountains trail community are divided. The obvious argument for reopening the old trail is to share the beauty of the cascades. The obvious argument against reopening is to protect a pristine spot from overuse and abuse.

If the area around Melville Cascades is as unspoiled as we believe it to be, and if a substantial increase in traffic would seriously damage the area, we vote strongly against reopening the trail. Is this depriving large numbers from a wonderful experience? Undoubtedly. If we are trying to prevent human impact, we cannot deny that large numbers will be deprived of seeing Melville Cascades.

The question we would ask next, however, is whether the hiking public is fast running out of interesting and inspiring places to visit. Not so! The overwhelming majority of Green Mountain hikers, even regular visitors, have not begun to exhaust all of the truly interesting and inspiring places currently accessibly by well-worn trails. Over in New Hampshire's White Mountains there are a lot more visitors, but even there we doubt if more than a handful of seasoned White Mountains hikers have come anywhere close to visiting all the beautiful spots accessible by trail.

The point is that places reached by trails can, in general, absorb a great deal more traffic without significantly greater impact. Little damage is done as more people visit Emerald Pool, Devil's Gulch, Sterling Pond, the Howks, Cantilever Rock, Nancy

Pond, Elephant's Head, Weetamoo Falls, the Subway, Spaulding Lake, Skylight Pond, or Ice Gulch—to pick almost at random a dozen marvelous and relatively little-visited spots reached easily by trails. If large numbers of White Mountain or Green Mountain hikers were growing bored with the existing trails and loudly demanding new ones, one might entertain a motion to reopen the trail to Melville Cascades. But this is plainly not the case.

Are we stirring up traffic to Melville Cascades by writing about that place in this book? Well, perhaps it has occurred to readers that we have changed the name, to protect the innocent. (Are you sure we even put it in the right state?) As outdoor writers we have long had to deal with the paradox of wanting to write about unspoiled places, yet thereby fostering an increase in visitors and an unacceptable impact on the most delicate microenvironments. Our solution, ever since we began writing, is that we either do not write about such places or else we are vague about location, change the name, confuse the account of how we got there.

Colin Fletcher, a far more widely read writer than we, copes with the problem in a similar manner:

> *Warning!* Do not be misled by any topographical information I give…. I have messed around with just enough of the facts to throw any would-be sleuth off the track…. I suppose I should also warn you that I am not above dragging plain red herrings across my page.
>
> I have practiced these obfuscations and deceits—and will continue to practice them, without notice or apology—because I am fearful that beautiful places I cherish may be violated by what I write…. You could say, I guess, that Heisenberg's Uncertainty Principle applies: if I describe a place, some people will be encouraged to go there and simply by going, will alter it.

Outdoor writers who keep their secrets may seem to be walking contradictions-in-terms, and are often subjected to a charge of selfishness; "elitism" is a favorite epithet. But, speaking for ourselves, it is not that we love our fellow humans less, but that we love those spots more. And anyway, we firmly believe that those who value these places deeply enough can and will find them on their own, by exploring, studying maps, considering the implications of terrain, peering discerningly from summit vistas. As we keep stressing, discovery is a major part of the experience of such places. We would not do anyone a favor by publishing all the secret places to the world.

We recognize one valid argument for reopening the trail, but it assumes a sequence of events that has not yet occurred. If word got around to the point that a very large number of hikers began to bushwhack up to Melville Cascades, they would begin to have an indiscriminate impact, which would be legitimate cause for concern. At some point, should the traffic increase, the only environmentally responsible solution would be to build a trail—or to designate the by-then-worn treadway as the authorized trail—and try to encourage the hiking traffic to keep to that trail. But if we ever reach that point, Melville Cascades will be a very different place. The experience of going there will be a very different experience. Much of the physical beauty will remain—not all, since the trail will alter some of the physical appearance—but the spirit of wildness will have been lost, where it is richly present now.

Meanwhile, to propose a trail to such places before the traffic has become large enough to have impact is to inflict a premature death on the spirit of wildness there. Listen to the warning of Robert Marshall, the prophet of American wilderness, east and west, theory and practice, at the policy level and on the ground:

> There are certain things that cannot be enjoyed by everyone. If everybody tries to enjoy them, nobody gets any pleasure out of them.

Melville Cascades is freely available to anyone who cares. It's a free country. Anyone can walk to Melville Cascades, with a little effort and bother. It's only a question of how much physical effort you're willing to pay for wildness.

If a trail goes in, it won't change the waterfall itself. It won't raise or lower the height, it won't alter the gallons per minute, nor the geology nor the latitude nor the longitude. But it will change how you see the falls. You will see that bare compacted rooty ground. You will notice the retreat of vegetation, of broken branches as people hang out to get a better look. In short, Melville Cascades will look like any other waterfall you pass on the trail or at a roadside picnic spot. That intense green, so pervasive it takes your breath away, that feeling of discovery, that rare rejoicing of spirit when you are in a truly wild spot—all this will be gone. Is that what anyone wants?

10

Trails and Wildness

There is a pleasure in the pathless woods,
There is a rapture on the lonely shore,
There is society, where none intrudes.
LORD BYRON, *CHILDE HAROLD'S PILGRIMAGE*

OFTEN HAVE WE STOOD on the top of Mount Lafayette in the
Franconia Range, gazing eastward over the rolling forests and
craggy ridges of the Pemigewasset Wilderness. The "Pemi" is an
extensive roadless area. Trails follow the chief valleys and
ridgelines. But much of that wilderness has no hiking trails. There
is no trail leading down off the Franconia Range into that magnificent area. As it says in the Wilderness Act, a wilderness is "an area
where the earth and its community of life are untrammeled by
man."

Not infrequently, on the summit of Lafayette, we have heard
someone—a companion of ours or a passing hiker we've struck up a
conversation with—express rapt admiration of this fine vista of
wildness. On two or three occasions, however, the observer has
gone on to comment: too bad there isn't a trail down off the ridge
directly into that area.

Wince. This wilderness and any wilderness gains much of its wild character precisely from being not that readily accessible. It is right that we should have to go the long way around, or undertake the trailless approach, or simply stand and watch and rejoice in its inaccessibility, honor the citadel left free to nature.

The cry of elitism is raised again. If there is no easily negotiable trail, then only the privileged few, those with great physical energy or experience, can enjoy the special privilege of visiting true wild country. This charge needs to be considered and evaluated.

One proposition that seems to command general support is that a popular mountain area should provide a spectrum of recreation experiences. Those who seek adventure and difficulty should be able to find it in the mountains. But if the area lies within a day's drive of millions of potential visitors, there should be easy access to many parts of it as well. Not everyone is a Reinhold Messner. The casual weekender, the elderly hiker, the children, the physically disabled should be able to enjoy a true backcountry experience. The key point is that a broad range of experiences be available.

Now one thing is absolutely certain. That is that the Green Mountains of Vermont and the White Mountains of New Hampshire afford rich opportunities for the casual weekender, the elderly hiker, the children, the physically limited. There is plenty of easy access. There are full-service huts in the backcountry. There are numerous easy trails. There are roads or gondolas or trains to each state's highest mountain. But apart from these especially heavy-handed means of access, there are plenty of foot trails so easy that almost anyone can walk to modest summits with breathtaking views, waterfalls, of incomparable beauty, and other scenic mountain locales; and so numerous that many such wonderful places see little traffic at all, though the trails are shown on maps, listed in guidebooks, and provided with trailhead parking and clear signposts.

When we suggest, as in the last chapter, that a trail should not be built to Melville Cascades, then, no one is about to deprive the elderly, the young, and the infirm of beautiful places to see. We are simply suggesting that some of those beautiful places remain accessible only by considerable effort.

If a full spectrum of experiences is to be available, then the rights of the physically hardy should be defended just as vigorously as the rights of the physically limited. It is illogical and unfair to agree that a broad range of experiences should be available, and then try to reduce every beautiful spot to universal access. There is little risk that the physically limited majority will run out of places to go. But there is serious risk, in the small and popular mountain areas of New England, that all ridges and valleys will be made so accessible that two tragic losses will occur: first, the opportunity for genuine adventure will be taken from those to whom the wild mountain world is especially precious; and second, the mountain environment will be exposed to excessive use levels, with unacceptable physical degradation.

Wild areas so close to the huge population centers of the East need some valleys and ridges with little human presence. They *can* be preserved—indeed, they have been, all through the 20th century, in spite of the burgeoning population just below the horizon to the south. A few ridges and valleys in the popular mountain areas of the Northeast are actually wilder today than they were in 1950. Hiking trails once cut through a number of wooded areas, trails now long abandoned and returned to nature. Everyone in the north country notes the expanding range of moose, bear, and coyote. Rumors increase about lynx, wolverine, even mountain lion. Such wonderful large mammals need vast tracts of land where they're unlikely to encounter people too often. If we all delight to think of large mammals coming back to our tiny beleaguered mountain world, then for heaven's sake, let's make that mental connection between their habitat requirements and our keeping some valleys inaccessible to people, trailless, not discussed in guidebooks. Is that relationship too difficult for us to perceive? Or don't we care enough? Do we consider our own self-indulgence as recreationists so important that it overrides the requirements of true wildness?

There is another point worth recalling. The spectrum of wilderness "users" is not static. Individual hikers, those who respond to increasing contact with the woods and hills, enjoy a process of expanding awareness, of personal growth, of progressively richer experiences. The first time any of us goes to the woods, we find them a bit scary. The first mountain climbed is exhausting. The first rainy day is decidedly unpleasant. As we return again and again, we learn more, we see more, and we develop our physical skills and, more important, our perception of the forest and mountain environment. If a flat three-mile walk to a waterfall seems like the extent of our powers the first year, we soon graduate to big mountains, steeper trails, more varied forest scenery. Let us hope we never lose our appreciation of that easily accessible waterfall. But let us surely hope that we develop a deeper understanding and appreciation of wild nature, and a growing capacity for different and more demanding experiences.

An incisive discussion of this "hierarchy of experience" appeared in a series of magazine articles by Philip D. Levin during the 1970s. Levin analyzed hiking and climbing as "a long apprenticeship." With a range of hiking or climbing experiences available, the hiker/climber may move up to greater difficulty and risk, and to less accessible goals, always with a sense "of better things yet to be attained." The process implies not only an improvement of physical skills but a broadening of the imagination and the will, a deepening appreciation of wilderness values, and a quickening of the spirit as well.

Thus, while wilderness is its own justification, it is also an incomparable medium for personal growth in those who respond to its call.

In a completely unrelated field, that of concert music, the pianist and writer Alfred Brendel has commended the best concert pianists for their "tough" programming, for publicly playing difficult and demanding modern pieces, on the following grounds: "Instead of playing down to an audience, the player should make the audience 'listen up.'" The analogy merits the attention of backcountry managers: instead of trying to make every corner of the backcountry available, should we not leave at least some difficult places to challenge the wilderness visitor to elevate his or her aspirations?

If wilderness plays such a dynamic, growing role for individuals, it is vital that we truly preserve that range of experience which meets the needs both of the novice and the fully committed. We must have trails and guidebooks and backcountry facilities to give the novice the opportunity to begin. But in the name of the mountain gods, let us also preserve some remote areas, difficult of access, demanding of their few visitors, so that those to whom the mountains have become a rich and integral part of their lives will always have their opportunities as well. A truly balanced view must acknowledge the need to retain the inaccessible and the difficult fully as much as the accessible and the easy. In Levin's words:

> When the mountains are made too accessible they become promiscuous and a violence is done to the natural ecosystem as well as to the human ecosystem.

III

MACHINES AMOK
IN THE GARDEN

Case Study

Scott, Hillary, and Ma Bell

*Radio, the magic sentinel, has watched over Admiral
Byrd and his men in the Antarctic since Dec. 28,
1928.... Radio, like an all-seeing eye, has enabled the
entire world to look into the Antarctic and even a few
miles beyond the South Pole.*

NEW YORK TIMES, FEBRUARY 9, 1930

ON APRIL 1, 1912, the *New York Times* carried the first in three
days of front-page headlines, news stories, and features concerning
the gallant bid of Robert Falcon Scott to reach the South Pole.
"SCOTT 150 MILES FROM SOUTH POLE JAN 3: WILL STAY IN ANTARCTIC
ANOTHER YEAR." A cable from New Zealand reported the arrival
there of Scott's support ship, the *Terra Nova*, bringing a message
from the intrepid expedition leader. From his tiny camp 150 miles
short of the Pole, Scott had sent three members of his party back
over the long ice journey, bringing his message to the ship at
McMurdo Sound. The *Terra Nova* then had to extricate itself from
the gathering pack ice before the Antarctic winter closed in.
Nearly three months after Scott sent his message, it finally appeared in newspapers.

Times readers thrilled to the account of Scott's adventure. None of them knew that, as they read, Scott and four others had perished just three days earlier in their storm-battered tent, only 11 miles short of the food cache with which they might have survived as heroes.

More than two months later, on June 16, 1912, two members of Scott's support team arrived in London. By this date Scott had lain dead for 80 days. His associates predicted success, expressing "confidence that Scott reached the pole about January 17."

On December 13, 1912—now more than nine months since the final disaster—the *Terra Nova* was reported leaving New Zealand to pick up the victorious captain at McMurdo Sound. The good ship was expected to touch base there by the second week of January, "when Captain Scott and his sledding party will probably be engaged in a journey of exploration to the southeast from the Beardmore Glacier."

At the time this December 13 story appeared, it had been more than a month since the overland relief expedition from the base of McMurdo Sound had discovered, on November 12, the lonely tent and its grisly contents of five corpses. The members of that relief team, however, who now knew the tragic outcome, were still isolated from the rest of the world in their lonely outpost at ice-choked McMurdo Sound. Readers of the *New York Times* still knew nothing about the disaster.

On February 4, 1913—more than 10 months since the death of her husband and almost 3 months since rescuers had found his remains—Mrs. Scott set sail for New Zealand "to meet her returning husband." Though having had no direct communication for 18 months, she told the press: "But I have no doubt whatsoever that he will arrive in New Zealand safely."

Less than a week later, a front-page notice in the *Times* carrying the headline "CAPT. SCOTT'S SHIP BACK" explained that the *Terra Nova* had been sighted reaching New Zealand. "It is believed the steamer brings back Capt. Scott and his party," said the *Times*, which went on to promise eager readers Scott's own personal account "as soon as it is received by cable, probably tomorrow morning."

The next day broke the news. Just 318 days after Scott and his men had died from starvation and exposure, a five-column headline told Americans: "SCOTT FINDS SOUTH POLE; THEN PERISHES WITH FOUR MEN IN ANTARCTIC BLIZZARD."

Recent revisionist historians have largely discredited Scott as hero material, but that is not our concern in bringing up the subject. Our point is this: During our own century, 80 years ago, news traveled so slowly from the Antarctic wastes that *New York Times* readers could be enthralled with the latest accounts of Scott's successes long after the poor man and his comrades lay dead, having failed to return from their quest. His own widow was at sea when the news broke, fully expecting to meet her returning hero, and did not learn of the catastrophe until long after the newspaper public.

Forty years later, in 1953, when Sir Edmund Hillary and Tenzing Norgay reached Everest's top for the first time, the coronation of the young Elizabeth II was about to take place, with all the pomp and pageantry of British monarchial tradition. The victorious Everesters reached the summit on May 29; the coronation was set for June 2. The night before the summit bid, huddled in a tent high in the West Cwm, expedition leader John Hunt had asked the British correspondent accompanying the expedition: "Supposing they climbed it, now, how soon d'you think you could get the news home to England? A week? Or less?" Through a supreme effort, the correspondent, James Morris, with the escort of climber Mike Westmacott, descended the treacherous Khumbu Icefall, then handed a coded message to a lanky young Nepalese runner, selected because he was extremely fast and reliable, who tore out over the Nepalese foothills and gorges to the nearest radio transmitter. Three days after the ascent, as the coronation pomp and procession began, the news broke in England and was broadcast through loudspeakers to cheering crowds along the coronation parade route.

In 1988 yet another team, this time American, was attempting the well-trodden challenge of the world's highest. In the intervening 35 years, progress in communications had soared

forward. These climbers became the first United States team to dial
directly home from Everest. And those at home could dial directly
to base camp. This team was in daily telephone contact with their
expedition headquarters in the United States, with the media, and
with those involved with their research projects.

From 318 days for Captain Scott...to four days for Hillary and
Tenzing...to direct dialing around the world from Everest base
camp—like calling next door.

The changes in communications in 75 years have done much
more than speed up the transmitting of news. They have erased a
yawning chasm or barrier of silence shrouding wilderness adventure
in mystery. Our vaunted technology has vaulted the void. Now we
have instant contact with the adventurers. And no mystery.

That void, that barrier of silence had a lot to do with the
quality of the adventure. When the early Antarctic explorers were
down there for months at a time, reliant entirely on their own
resources, completely out of touch, the experience had a spirit that
will never be found again on this planet, now that radio and air
support are available. Himalayan climbers reaching summits just
one generation ago were similarly out of touch up there. For them
the gulf between the hustle of civilization and the private intensity
of their ordeal was a rich gift.

Easy for us to say, you think. We who sit inside at our type-
writer before a warm wood stove may talk glibly of romantic
adventure on Antarctic wastes or Himalayan summits with no
avenue to outside contact or rescue. True, perhaps, but we have
sought what little adventure we can find in the small wilds of road-
ringed New England mountains. Some of these miniadventures are
mentioned elsewhere in these pages. The reader may have our
word that being out of touch with the outside world—even where
genuine risk is involved—is a vital part of the experience. Not a
small added spice, but a vital ingredient, an essential condition to
adventure, a sine qua non for the spirit of wildness.

Sure, we know, if you ask that American Everest team about
this point now, they'd tell you how wonderful it was to talk with
loved ones back home. If you asked Hunt in 1953, he bloody well

would have wished for some way to get the news to his queen in time for the coronation. Had you asked Scott, he'd have opted for a quick rescue rather than die in silence on the frozen waste. If technology is there, we use it, no questions asked.

But what else do we get when we have instant communication? And what do we lose? What element of romance is destroyed, not only for the spectators but for the participants?

In 1985 a small team of adventurers walked across the Antarctic continent to the South Pole, calling their expedition "In the Footsteps of Scott." They wanted to honor this great explorer; but more to the point, they wanted, in this age of instant communication, to experience the isolation Scott felt. They took no radio, made no link of backup bases, hauled every ounce of food and fuel for a march of 883 miles across the most dangerous and unspoiled landscape in the world. Contrived? Perhaps. But these modern explorers sought the precious and beleaguered quality of isolation. To find it they went to the last great wilderness left on Earth.

Those readers who are in their teens or twenties perhaps weren't born when Neil Armstrong first set foot on the moon. Those who are in their thirties and forties vividly recall watching on television the historic step. But those of us in our fifties and sixties, let alone our elders, recall not only Armstrong's day of glory, but also the science fantasies of Buck Rogers and others only a couple of decades before manned moon flights, when many writers speculated on what it would be like. A lot of the fantasy was remarkably prophetic. Space suits of the 1960s sort of looked like Buck's outfit of the 1940s. The big rockets blasted off rather like they had in the comic books 20 years earlier.

But do you know what was different? What was the single thing that almost none of the fantasy dreamers got right? What was the one element in Neil Armstrong's actual landing and walk that was *not* anticipated by the fiction writers? The one point that, in the reality, proved totally and significantly different from all the fantasies of humanity's first moon landing?

It was that *at the very moment it happened, we were all watching it on television.* Blurry and a bit puzzling, but there was the image on the home screen, of the ladder down from the landing capsule to the gravelly surface of the moon, with Armstrong's space-suited foot touching down before our very eyes.

This was just 57 years after Scott had lain for the better part of a year with his fate unknown. Communications technology has invaded the sphere of adventure, pushed the once-solitary individual or close-knit group into a walk-on role for television.

11

Radio and Wildness

Noise is the most impertinent of all forms of interruption. It is not only an interruption, but also a disruption of thought.

ARTHUR SCHOPENHAUER, *STUDIES IN PESSIMISM*

NOW BRING THE question back from the far-off moon or the Antarctic, to somewhere closer to home, some place we can all visualize with more personal immediacy. What are the effects of improved communications in those islands of wildness closer to home?

In the White Mountains of New Hampshire, at the Appalachian Mountain Club's high mountain huts, there was a time—as late as the 1960s—when radio contact was intermittent and unreliable. Recreationists spending the night up in the mountains had essentially no way of transmitting a message to the valley any faster than a willing and speedy hut man could race down the rocky trail and personally report that message. The crew operating the hut was on its own to handle any situation that came up. When you spent the night at a hut, anything might happen in the outside world and you'd never know it till you came out of the hills a day or several days later. In fact, you didn't care what was happening in the outside world.

Radio aficionado Alex McKenzie has lovingly related the story of how improvements in radio technology have gradually made "better" communication possible. In 1976 "consistent communication" between Pinkham and each of the eight high huts became a reality. In 1984 further improvements greatly improved the reliability and flexibility of the system.

Now each morning after breakfast AMC headquarters in the valley speaks directly with the crew of each hut. Changes in reservations are reported, late weather reports disclosed; any changes in shuttle bus arrangements for picking up the guests at the trailhead can be arranged on a daily basis.

No one would think of dismantling this radio network. The practical administrators who manage the hut system would tell you that the modern huts could not operate without it. They're right, of course.

But one of us served on the AMC's Huts Committee when those 1970s radio arrangements were first proposed, and we recall clearly that the committee did not receive the proposal with unalloyed enthusiasm. At least some members of the committee voiced the question, Why do people go to the huts? High up there in the mountains, do they *want* to know they're in touch with the valley? Or did they go up into the mountains precisely so they could get out of communication with the valley? Don't we speak of vacations as "getting away from it all?"

Down on the edges of the backcountry, at drive-in campgrounds, national parks, scenic roadside vistas, the publicly aired radio has pretty much won the day. But no one with any sensitivity for the outdoor world is happy about it. The western outdoor writer Patrick McManus explains:

Many people are under the mistaken impression that transistor radios come from Japan, but that is not the case. Transistor radios breed in national parks and from there move out to infest the rest of the country. Their mating cries at night are among the most hideous sounds on earth. The offspring are prodigious in number.

McManus proposed a hunting season on radios with an eye to limiting population growth, but found park officials, while sympathetic, powerless to act.

Up in the backcountry, radios are still not viewed generally as appropriate. There are disquieting signs of change, however.

It is less and less a novelty to meet hikers high in the hills strolling along with an earphone and wire leading to a radio or tape player or whatever the latest electronic marvel is termed. Fortunate indeed to meet an earphone rather than a boom box directly transmitting its contents to the open air, but you meet those too, less often. It is baffling and frustrating to hear a radio in the mountains, whether playing rock or Bach. Yet we know mountaineers with apparent love of climbing who, parked in a remote dirt-road-accessed campground, will switch on the car radio or tape deck. Whether they send a Brandenburg concerto to the surrounding woods or heavy metal makes little difference to the spirit of the occasion.

You could get a lot of support for turning off radios in the woods. A large number of backcountry travelers, very likely a majority, would say that the noise is inappropriate or at least an inexcusable intrusion on the experience of those for whom that sound is an offense. It's a good thing people feel that way. As of now, at least, the proponents of hearing someone else's radio on a mountaintop are small.

But is noise the issue? Only partly. Much more important than the intrusion of noise is the intrusion of a tie back to the world of technology and civilization. Now, civilization is not a bad thing—don't be ridiculous, civilization's a blessing, a proud achievement of the species, and the Brandenberg concertos are one of the brightest manifestations of civilized culture. But what are we doing on a mountaintop? Seeking civilization, however brightly manifested? Or are we there precisely to cut that tie? Apparently it's a hard tie for some of us to cut.

Recently we snowshoed a trail in to a waterfall to practice ice climbing. The spray had frozen as it dropped and now all was crystalline, a looming mass of hard water ice, broad, glassy, sheer. Once turbulent motion, it was now stilled in immobile grandeur.

While we were climbing, several hiking parties walked in, also to admire the winter waterfall. No one stayed long. Well into the afternoon, a final party arrived with backpacking gear to set up a tent in a flat area below the falls, as we watched from above on the ice. At one point we descended for a late lunch, and this camping party came over, interested in our ice-climbing gear. We all talked about the delight and peace one could find in the mountains in winter. We went back up for one last climb, they to their comfortable-looking camp.

Soon we heard…was it really?…unfortunately, yes…the clear sounds of…music. We looked down and saw a very large piece of electronic equipment on the snow near the tent. A tape deck? Ghetto blaster? We couldn't be sure. Out of consideration for others (us) it was not turned up loud. But we were surprised at how well that intrusive sound carried up to us. We found it hard to concentrate on the climbing as the unwelcome noise followed us all the way up the ice. We left soon after this, not saying anything to those music lovers. Perhaps we should have. Perhaps we should have pointed out how at odds with the wild beauty of the ice tower above them was this piece of civilization they'd gone to great trouble to carry in. But it's hard to do this sort of thing and not sound like a killjoy, preachy.

A friend of ours reported recently encountering a hiking party, miles from the road, in which one member had a video camera on his shoulder. Reported our friend:

> I couldn't see if it was turned on, recording for the folks back home every rock of the Bondcliff Trail. I can see it coming: videos, rentable at your local store, of all the trails, step by step, rock by rock, panning for views now and then. Then, of course, the next step will be bushwhack videos; see what it's

like to go to Carrigain Pond, from the comfort of your arm-
chair VCR operated by remote control.

To the operator of that video camera and perhaps to his friends,
here was a big advance in technological progress. How nice to be able
to play back at home that great day on the Bond range. Anyone
objecting must seem not only antiprogress but antifun as well.

Our friend mentioned Carrigain Pond. Let us tell you a story
about Carrigain Pond. This is a quiet, indescribably beautiful
wilderness pond ringed by very dense spruce-fir forest and steep,
rugged mountain slopes. It's a long ways in by New England
wilderness standards—four miles from the nearest gravel road, and
several hours' bushwhack from any trail, which may not sound like
a long distance by western standards, and isn't, but the terrain
involved makes it no easy destination for most hikers.

On one occasion six of us bushwhacked into Carrigain Pond
from the south. We took about eight hours to get there, walking
first on abandoned wood roads, then crashing through the dense
saplings in a freshly logged area of hardwoods, contouring along a
steep-sloping coniferous forest, across one open rock slide, then up
steeply through rock outcroppings, over a height-of-land, and then
down through moose-infested small conifers to the quiet shores of
this jewel of a pond. There, at three o'clock in the afternoon, we
consulted on how to get back out with safety. We decided that to
retrace our steps in would be not simply arduous but perhaps so
time consuming that we'd risk being benighted before reaching
ground that we could negotiate in the dark. The alternative we
selected was to go up 1,600 feet of steep mountainside, through
increasingly dense, stunted forest, in order to reach the summit of
Mount Carrigain, whence we could be assured of a well-marked
hiking trail all the way out to our cars. This meant a tough couple
of hours, and we were already tired, but it also meant a clear way
out should we be overtaken by night. So up we thrashed, arriving
on the incomparable summit of Carrigain at about five o'clock.

Here, overlooking the rich vista of wilderness country,
basking in the reflection of a day's strenuous exertions, far from any

hint of the works of humanity, tired from our labors but immensely happy with the sights and sounds, the feelings and comradeship of the day, one member of the party pulled out...a radio! Or something of that ilk, on which he called home and spoke with his wife—hon, we're on the top of Carrigain now, we should be out by, oh, around eight, and I'll probably be home around quarter to nine.

Nothing against this individual, who is one of the nicest gentlemen you could meet and who truly loves the White Mountains. But right at that moment, what did the radio do? Yes, it let his wife know we were safe and what time to expect us. But it did a lot more than that. It whispered to us that we'd never really been in wilderness all day. We had made no commitment to rely on our own resources. Had there been trouble, the radio could have speedily summoned rescue. Did all this ruin the day? Of course not. That was a wonderful hike into Carrigain Pond, one of our nicest memories. But something changed the minute that radio came out.

Remember Abbey's Analogy: would you play a radio in a cathedral? In the middle of communion, would you dial home to tell your wife when the service would be over?

To repeat, it's not just the noise. On another occasion, the same gentleman who carried the radio to Carrigain Pond started off on another bushwhack with us and told us he was (a) planning to take his two-way radio, but (b) would keep it turned off, so we wouldn't be bothered by it. Well, heck, this fellow is such a sweet guy, no one's going to tell him he can't bring along his toy. But the fact that we don't hear it is not much of a point. Take that back; it helps, a lot. But the fact remains that the radio is there, a tie to what we wanted to leave behind, a relentless reminder that we emphatically have not left our civilization or its technology, that we are in touch if we "need" to be, and whether we like it or not.

Cellular telephones pose a future threat to wildness that should be taken seriously right now. We may be too late. In the Angeles National Forest, a California hiker got lost, so he simply whipped out his cellular phone and called his wife. The good woman then phoned the Forest Service, which dispatched a helicopter to the rescue. Will this story be repeated with growing frequency?

Appalachian Trail hikers have proposed "signs in every shelter with the telephone number to call and the quickest way to get to a phone in an emergency." In the backcountry? Is it not a short step from there to a cellular phone "booth" at every shelter?

Perhaps the most bizarre case of all was the lost hiker who was carrying a battery-powered TV and, for several days, watched reports of rescuers looking for him. Incredible!

Where does all this lead us? Is it just hand-wringing over the inevitable march of technology? Nostalgia for a past that can never be recalled? Would we try to turn the clock back (or the clock-radio)? Would we join King Canute sitting on the beach, trying to command the tide of technology to recede?

These are reasonable questions, and they must be faced. Change is inevitable. History deals harshly with idle dreamers who cannot accept and adjust to change. The Luddites throwing wooden shoes into the textile machines did not stop the tide of industrialization.

But with the mountain experience, we can and do make choices. We all (or most of us, surely anyone caught turning these pages) agree that roads should not be brought into the mountains. Most agree that we don't want electric lights, television, and other comforts of the electronic age at a backcountry shelter. We have no hesitation in resisting change in these areas, in denying the fruits of "progress," in rejecting technology in at least some spheres. Why? Because we are trying to preserve a certain kind of experience in the backcountry. We deliberately and calmly reject some forms of technology in order to preserve a spirit of wildness. We light candles at an altar; we don't just switch on a battery of electric lights.

So the question is, How much technology do we reject and how much do we accept for the backcountry? How much "inevitable" change do we decide we can and will keep out of the mountains?

It becomes a matter of deciding which forms of technology are appropriate to the mountain experience. We are not trying to turn back technology in the cities. There, we say, it's appropriate. But, we ask, how much technology is appropriate in the backcountry?

What disturbs us is a growing suspicion that a lot of others out there on the hiking trails, along the high mountain ridges, and even within the leadership positions of major hiking clubs are not asking these questions. Do they feel deeply that there are limits to technology in the backcountry? Are they oblivious to the impact of technological toys on the spirit of wildness?

Thoughtful students of technology's larger social implications, such as Langdon Winner, the author of *The Whale and the Reactor: A Search for Limits in an Age of High Technology*, are asking: "What forms of technology are compatible with the kind of society we want to build?" We should, in our narrower sphere, be asking the corresponding question: What forms of technology are compatible with the kind of backcountry experience we want to preserve?

When a new technology is applied to the backcountry, we tend to focus on its practical uses. When someone later points out a new gadget's impact on the quality of the wilderness experience, we tend to classify such ramifications as "secondary" or "side effects" of the technology's application. By taking this view, we preclude questioning the original, intended use of the technology. But in fact the changes that a new technology makes on the wilderness experience are not at all secondary, but are intrinsic to the very nature of that technology. The medium *is* the message. The tool *becomes* the experience.

Can we not reach a new consensus that the spirit of wildness is more important than the convenience of backcountry managers, the titillation of hikers themselves, or even some elusive added measure of safety? We don't seek to turn back the clock, but we emphatically would like to turn people's thinking just a bit more toward respect for the wild mountain experience.

Shall we be more specific? OK, about radios: we would love to see the day:

- When you never, literally never, hear a commercial or public radio broadcast, or tape deck, or the equivalent, in the backcountry. Neither Bach nor rock. No weather forecasts. No Celtics playoff.

- When you walk into a backcountry off-road shelter of any kind, you never hear a radio or tape.
- When each ham radio or CB buff voluntarily decides that, as much fun as his toy gives him at home or on the road, it just doesn't belong in the backcountry, and he'll always leave it at home when he goes off to the mountains.
- When you hear a CB radio, walkie-talkie, or any other form of squawk box, it turns out to be a ranger, shelter caretaker, or other official backcountry manager on official business, or perhaps a search-and-rescue mission.
- When rangers, or anyone else carrying radios, refrain from leaving the receiving end routinely on.
- When you attend a committee or board meeting of any outdoor organization, you never hear anyone propose to extend the sphere of radio contact in the backcountry; and if any individual does raise the issue, five to seven other committee members stomp all over the very idea.
- When winter climbers, or parties penetrating more remote areas in summer, accept the genuine risk that they are on their own to handle all emergencies; to be their own sole resource for rescue (self-rescue); to have no way of letting anyone else know what's happening by means of the airwaves. Risk? Certainly.

Are we making too much of a harmless little electronic gadget or two? What we're trying to say is that it's much more than a gadget. The toy takes over any scene it's a part of. The mountains are not the place for communication with civilization. The spirit of wildness asks us to leave the radio at home.

We close with an opinion voiced by the poet William Cowper in 1785:

> O for a lodge in some vast wilderness,
> Some boundless contiguity of shade,
> Where rumor of oppression and deceit,
> Of unsuccessful or successful war,
> Might never reach me more.

Case Study

The Saga of the Snowmobile

Few things are harder to put up with
than the annoyance of a good example.
MARK TWAIN

OUR NEXT CHAPTER, where we talk about the proliferation of one-person transportation devices and their impact on wildness, is going to be on the pessimistic side. To counteract the gloom, and to show that we're not really nattering nabobs of negativism with respect to *all* forms of off-road mechanized transport, let's talk quietly first about one machine that has often been loudly condemned by pedestrian lovers of the backcountry: the snowmobile.

The snowmobile was perhaps the first important new one-person transportation device to enter the backcountry after World War II. For the townsfolk of north country villages, who previously faced three months of boredom between hunting season and sugaring, the snowmobile was a release, a blessing. That's no small gain for an important segment of north country society.

But for the spirit of wildness it was another story. For a while some of us thought that was curtains for winter silence and solitude. Those snow machines brought noise and human presence to remote places that formerly had been silent and lonely from November to April. Vast chunks of seasonal wildness were irretrievably altered. There is no way to turn the clock back to the time when the farthest outbacks saw unbroken snow cover for miles in every direction. That much is pure loss.

But then a lot of good things began to happen. Backcountry managers wisely recognized that winter recreationists had to be given clearly delineated places to play. Snowmobiles were given plenty of room to roam, but rigidly excluded from other places, reserved for the older, slower, quieter forms of winter travel. On the positive side, snowmobile clubs became a vocal and effective lobby for the preservation of large tracts of roadless areas. In Maine conservationists credit the clubs with a key role in keeping the north woods remote, though not quiet when their machines were out there. But the snowmobilers weren't able to go everywhere, and eventually they proved willing to curb their voracious appetite for acreage. In many places, snowmobile clubs became effective forces in herding their members on to designated snowmobile trails and keeping them off other places.

The results are by no means perfect. Many large tracts of wilderness or parklands, where it would have been nice to keep a quiet world, have been invaded by battalions of snowmobiles. Once snowmobile routes have been used a few years, the drivers begin to feel they belong there. Dartmouth College has the responsibility for the beautiful but fragile summit area of Mount Moosilauke, but all its efforts, including large, plainly worded, very polite signs, have not stopped the machines from roaring over the tundra up there regularly.

Nevertheless, in many areas the hoped-for division of the backcountry has worked remarkably well. In the White Mountain National Forest, the snowmobiles have been granted certain "corridors" and been asked to stay off other trails. It works pretty well: it is very seldom that the winter climber will find his backwoods idyll interrupted by engine noise.

When we first moved to a wooded Vermont hillside almost 20 years ago, we had about one "snowmobile incident" each winter for about 5 years. Then such encounters ceased. For well over 10 years now, no snowmobile has crossed our land. This has been a surprise to us, and a pleasant one. Apparently two things have happened. One is that local snowmobilers know we're there, know we're not fond of the sound of motors, and respect our rights. That's not just most of the local folks; that's *every one* of them. The other thing is that Vermont has a respected organization called Vermont Association of Snow Travelers (VAST), which has worked out a lengthy and varied trail system for its members, carefully securing landowner permission, and (very important) educating its members in a strong ethic about respecting landowner rights and not leaving the trails.

A related development, also a surprise to us, is that snowmobiles of the 1990s really are a lot quieter than those of the 1970s. We never thought that would happen. We assumed that a whole lot of noise was part of the thrill in the sport. But somehow the industry and its customers seem to have accepted a lot of restraint on the noise level. That certainly helps. Boy, those first machines were loud. Today it's possible to have one ride by without going temporarily deaf.

In recent years we've varied our routine of winter climbing in the White Mountains with a few backyard excursions to some of the small, unspectacular wooded 3,000-footers nearby in Vermont. We've noticed an interesting point. To reach these little peaks we often use a snowmobile trail up through a pass, then strike off through unbroken snow to the top on our snowshoes. As a result we encounter passing parades of snowmobiles, in groups ranging from 2 or 3 to 15 or 20. There is *always* a friendly wave and a smile. Not infrequently one or more snowmobilers will stop to chat. These are invariably friendly meetings. Those folks aren't accustomed to seeing people on foot and sometimes their first question is whether we're in trouble and need a ride. After that we often exchange thoughts about our different styles of enjoying the outdoors, but it's always in a pleasant vein. At least so far that's our experience.

We suppose that the relatively low level of use in the Vermont hills, together with our mutual acknowledgment that we're both guests on private lands, helps. Maybe on public lands both groups of recreationists feel they have rights that the other is jeopardizing.

Anyway, we bring the illustration of snowmobiles up because our experience has been that it *is* possible to work out separate domains or coexistence for what seems to be mutually incompatible uses. Therefore, it *is* possible to accommodate revolutionary new technology without devastating older, slower, quieter winter recreation. The saga of the snowmobile is worth recalling when we turn to consider all their summertime cousins: the proliferation of one-person transportation devices.

12

One-Person Transportation Devices and Wildness

*Every joy that life gives must be earned ere it is secured:
and how hardly earned, those only know who have
wrestled for great prizes. The heart's blood must gem with
red beads the brow of the combatant before the wreath of
victory rustles over it.*

CHARLOTTE BRONTË, *SHIRLEY*

RECENTLY THREE CLIMBERS pioneered a new route on a huge
north face in the Canadian Rockies. Their route was difficult and
demanding, and they reached the summit with daylight nearly
gone. At that point two of them located the hikers' trail that goes
down the easy side, but were soon benighted and groped down the
rocky footway, reaching their car five wearying hours later. The
third climber? While the three sat on the summit watching the
impending sunset, he dug into his pack, unfolded his parapente,
and sailed off, reaching the car in a bit over 10 minutes.

Obviously times have changed for mountain climbers. Remember those long harrowing descents we read about, of the French in 1950 coming off Annapurna? Hermann Buhl spending the night by himself just below the top of Nanga Parbat? Willy Unsoeld reciting Robert Frost as he prepared to bivouac just off the summit of Everest? If there's much more progress in one-person flying devices, such epics will soon be the stuff only of bygone legends. Perhaps the modern world has little use for epic. Who reads Homer when they can watch Bill Cosby?

Recent technological change in one-person transportation devices may have more impact on the wilderness spirit than anything else we've been talking about in these pages. Can humanity process such change and still retain the spirit of wildness in the backcountry? We profoundly hope so, but it is not going to be easy.

We have just shown that we at least find a glimmer of hope in the saga of the snowmobile. We are far less optimistic in contemplating the more recent proliferation of summertime one-person transportation devices. Are we prophets of doom? Let us review the prospects.

The devices in question fall into three categories, with distinct issues involved. First the motorized all-terrain vehicles of summer, whose distinguishing feature is a lot of noise and usually a lot of unmistakable impact on the land. A second category is the mountain bike, with no motor, no noise, and considerably less physical effect on many, though probably not all, backcountry environments. A third is the soaring or flying device, the hang gliders, parapentes, hovercraft, and who knows what else, which are absolutely certain to be developed into practical application within a few years.

ATVs

The issues involved with motorized all-terrain vehicles most closely approximate those of snowmobiles—but with a significant difference. Their noise and physical impact make their incompatibility with wilderness values patently obvious. As a result, it is not going to take much of a fight to keep them out of a substantial share of the truly wild backcountry. Not that there won't be abuses and territorial disputes. In the West some vocal ATV groups are putting a lot of pressure on land managers to open more trails for their use. But it should be possible to win some of those fights and persuade a majority that ATVs have to be excluded from any place where wilderness values are prized.

Unfortunately, the analogy with snowmobiles isn't perfect. Operating on a cover of snow, the winter vehicle doesn't directly tear up the land, and the indirect effects, while not negligible, can be tolerated in most areas. Not so with the summertime ATVs. Sad to say, there is almost no place for these machines to go—that is, no place where their drivers want to go—where they won't have a sizable impact. Drivers of these machines seek the feeling of power the comes with getting up steep hills and sloshing through muddy ground. You see it in the advertisements, which show the machines throwing dirt, mud, and water as they roar over the land. The snowmobiler can whip up a trail of powder snow behind him and in the spring nothing's changed; the ATV chewing up a hillside or gouging through a mud slough is scarring the land tragically and, for all practical purposes, permanently.

We have had ATVs slice noisily through our woods. The experience is not a happy one. Our instinct for neighborliness and accommodation of diverse recreation makes us want to say: please don't drive there or there, but you're welcome to go here and here. The trouble is there is *no* place they *can* go where they don't seriously impact the land. The only impervious surfaces in our part of the world are paved or very well-worn wood roads. But those places have little appeal to the ATV operator. The whole point of the ATV is that it *can* go on "all terrain." If you want to drive well-worn wood roads you take your pickup. The ATV is meant to traverse ground unavailable to regular vehicles—yet just about all such ground is distressingly vulnerable to its impact.

For those reasons wilderness areas, whether they be officially designated wildlands or any other reasonably wild backcountry tracts, cannot tolerate ATV abuse, and backcountry managers know that. Fights there will be, but the cause of wildness should be able to win some of those fights.

Mountain Bikes

The mountain bikes present an entirely different image and impact level. You don't find many hikers or backpackers roaring around on ATVs, but a lot of hiking and climbing friends we know have taken to mountain bikes with enthusiasm. There's almost no noise—maybe even less than a hiker's footsteps—and in many kinds of terrain there's little physical impact. Many people we respect feel that mountain bikes are perfectly compatible in hiking country, that they are simply an alternative way of being in the quiet backcountry, one that many hikers will prefer on relatively easy-grade trails.

Our instinct is to want to say, fine. Welcome, mountain bikers, have fun. If we can tolerate snow machines on our Vermont hills, surely we can have no objection to mountain bikes.

Maybe it's that simple, but then again maybe it isn't. If you recall the October trip to Lake Wietelmann that we described in part 2 of this book, we'd like to tell you about a conversation the five of us had on the way out. When we regained the trail after bushwhacking down from Lake Wietelmann, it was late in an October day, destined to grow dark soon, and we were still six and a half miles from the road. The trail was relatively level, certainly terrain a skillful rider could manage easily on a mountain bike. We talked a good deal about how it would be to have biked in to that point and cached our bikes in the woods, so we could bike out now. Figure that it took us three hours to walk in and about that long, when tired at the end of the day, to walk out. That's six hours spent trudging along a largely uninspiring trail, just so we could enjoy perhaps five hours of bushwhacking and being at Lake Wietelmann. On bikes, what might that take: half an hour in, a bit less out? Wouldn't that improve the day considerably: six hours, not eleven; or, alternatively, much more time to enjoy Lake Wietelmann?

Many mountain bikers feel that this ease of access is a compelling point. Mike Usen, writing in *Appalachia Bulletin*, calls mountain bikes "an efficient means of accessing nature," and points out: "Best of all, [the mountain bike] offers seemingly instant access to the beauty and serenity of the trails and wooded areas."

That rationale is going to look awfully attractive to a lot of people. To probe deeper requires thinking through once more the question we've been asking throughout this book: *What are we trying to preserve?* Just the physical act of getting to the backcountry? Or the process of getting there? Are the three-hour trudge in and the three-hour trudge out part of what brings us to Lake Wietelmann?

Not everyone likes the idea of "instant access" to wilderness. One concerned observer puts it this way:

> One of my greatest concerns with mountain bikes is the effect they have on remoteness. What was an overnight march becomes an easy day-ride, and with the transformation comes not only an increase in numbers but also a difference in the quality of a place.

In 1992 the Appalachian Trail Conference expressed concern about the impact of mountain bikes on the Appalachian Trail and called for government agencies to close the AT to mountain bikes with exceptions where (1) stretches of trail were previously designed for wheeled vehicles, (2) trail sections are part of established multiple-use trails, (3) vehicles can be physically restricted to a designated path, and (4) mountain bikes "would not adversely affect the recreational experience of hikers."

As this book is written, the issue of mountain bikes is still evolving rapidly. Their role in the backcountry is not yet well defined. Whether they will ultimately prove to fit smoothly and pleasantly into the scheme of things, or whether they become a source of friction and division in the ranks of wilderness lovers, has not been worked out.

What the issue underscores is an unfortunate tendency in modern backcountry management to categorize all of us in "user groups." It is not just the managers' fault. Organized segments of our recreation industry have evolved a view of backcountry that focuses on "use" rather than more subtle and enduring values. Thereby we are all lumped into categories of "user groups," and our "interests" are to be balanced according to whether we are day hikers or backpackers or mountain bikers or skiers or whatever. But when it comes to wilderness, this very concept of "use" steers our thinking into counterproductive channels. One does not "use" the wilderness. Wilderness is more than a physical location, and visitors to wilderness should not be perceived as just another category of recreationists, to be counted and managed. Wilderness values should be meaningful to all "users" of the mountains and the backcountry. Whoever we are, and however we came to the land, remoteness and difficulty of access should be part of a wilderness experience.

But where do you draw the line? During our discussion walking out from Lake Wietelmann, we asked, What about cross-country skiing? We two happen to be snowshoers; we don't own a pair of cross-country skis. Do we complain because skiers can reach remote sites several times easier and quicker than snowshoers? As a practical matter, we've never felt the slightest resentment of skiers in the backcountry. So what's wrong with bikes, a summertime version of getting there a lot quicker and easier? Why do we react differently? The answer to that question is party historical: skis have been a traditional medium for backcountry travel since long before we began—hundreds and hundreds of years in some places. It is our own choice that we do not avail ourselves of skis, but settle for plodding out those level trails at two miles per hour instead of floating out at eight (or whatever it would be). But that's only part of the answer. The mountain biker says: look, no motor. True, we say, but there is definitely a mechanical advantage. The bike is a machine. A sense of the invasion of remote places comes whenever you see any kind of machine in the backcountry, quiet or not. If you were out in the woods with tools and time, you could make skis. You couldn't make a bike. Are these significant differences?

With an issue that is still in a state of rapid evolution, it's not so important to be certain of answers to these questions right now. It is important, though, to keep thinking about them. Neither friends nor foes of mountain bikes should respond defensively with easy answers to difficult questions. The mountain bike is a good case study of what's at stake in wilderness: What are our fundamental values? What are we trying to preserve?

One-Person Flying Machines

Here's another way to look at it, and this brings us to the third category of summertime one-person transportation devices. If all we want to do is get to the shores of Lake Wietelmann (or any other remote backcountry setting), why stop with a mountain bike for the on-trail portion of the trip? Make no mistake, the technology will soon be here for soaring or gliding or hovering (or something) to anywhere we choose. Already you can hike or climb to the nearest mountaintop, then hang-glide or parapente your way safely down to any spot where a landing is feasible. Soon the technology won't even require being higher than your destination, given the right wind currents and some experience at the art.

At that point it's Katie, bar the door. Talk about "instant access"! What is left of the concept of wildness or wilderness when access becomes that easy? Is wildness truly dead at that point?

We don't know. One thing we're sure of: don't take too much comfort about today's state of the art. It may well be that the current flying machines can't really reach Lake Wietelmann, that the wind has to be just right, that bad weather keeps wild areas inaccessible. But the way technology is progressing, and the way some hikers and climbers are eagerly embracing the latest gadgets, it is absolutely certain that one-person airborne devices will progress rapidly. The day will soon be here of the nightmare of universal accessibility to anywhere save the largest expanses of wilderness.

Sorry to end on a pessimistic note, but we see no good way out. The only solution we see is the tenuous road of self-restraint. Abbey's Analogy again: you just don't fly up the nave of a cathedral, nor do you ride a quiet mountain bike along the aisle, even if it would get you in and out quicker and leave more time for prayers. Backcountry managers may outlaw airborne devices, but that's going to be uniquely difficult to enforce when the offender can take off and glide back to town. Our impression of some of today's parapente artists is that they view their feat as an expression of personal freedom and reject all restraints, even to the point of laughing about their ruses for avoiding arrest. Climbers in Yosemite Valley are greatly tickled by the illegal parachute jumps off El Capitan, and it's become a huge joke to see who can outwit the frustrated rangers.

Freedom in the wild is a legitimate aspect of the spirit of wildness. But as the old Dutch domini who married us 20 years ago once said, when reflecting on his efforts to understand and be sympathetic with changing modern values: we all need a lot of humility in trying to understand other viewpoints, but there comes a time when you just have to say, "Thus saith the Lord!"

Trying to stop the application of technology may be difficult in the area of communication devices, but is it even possible in the area of transportation devices? We can only hope that humanity's vision of the technologically possible can be matched by humanity's vision of the value of maintaining the spirit of wildness. Beyond that, as the Count of Monte Cristo counseled, all we can do is: Wait and Hope.

13

Aircraft and Wildness

To those travelling there on foot, a helicopter flying by
does more than ruin the ambience of the moment. Its
presence symbolizes that no place is safe from our
excessive ways.

GREAME POLE

NEVADA IS THE Sagebrush State. It's the seventh largest of the 50 states territorially, but one of the 4 or 5 smallest in population. These wide-open spaces are home to single-leaf pinion trees, mountain bluebirds, and the armed forces of the United States. More than 4 million acres of Nevada are allotted to military activity. Fully 70 percent of the state's airspace is assigned to "Special Use Airspace" and Military Training Routes. A few years ago the Air Force proposed to fuse three large Nevada training sites into one Continental Operations Range (COR). While the plan was temporarily blocked in Congress, advocates remained hopeful: "Eventually, I think we are going to get there," said the director of operations of one of the three bases, with reference to COR. We are glad we live in New England.

We've never hiked in Nevada, but like a lot of others we've been in so-called wilderness areas when Air Force training jets flew over in close formation. The effect on the wilderness experience needs no mention. "You're communing with nature," said one visitor to Utah's canyonlands, "and all of a sudden a huge symbol of our military-industrial complex comes screaming low overhead."

In New Mexico, Holloman Air Force Base sends 350 to 400 flights per day over White Sands National Monument. Over Washington's Olympic National Park, two different military operations regularly train through the air space.

Nor are the military by any means the sole offenders. In 1989 a special report by a task force of the Society of American Foresters found that other agencies of the federal government were far too casual in dispatching aircraft over the quiet backcountry:

> Land-management agencies have tried to curtail unnecessary flights in wilderness, but other agencies, like the U.S. Geological Survey, Federal Aviation Administration, Environmental Protection Agency, Soil Conservation Service, and fish and wildlife agencies have not. Insensitive to the effects on wilderness, these agencies frequently seek permission to use aircraft as a quick, expedient means of travel when other methods could accomplish their objectives just as well. Likewise organizers of search-and-rescue operations are also quick to use aircraft and helicopters, even in situations that are not life-threatening.

Nor are government agencies the only culprits. In fact, when it comes to natural scenic areas, low-flying commercial aircraft loaded with gawking tourists are probably a bigger problem. At Devil's Tower a sightseeing company runs 20 to 30 flights per day at elevations as low as 200 to 1,300 feet. The Federal Aviation Administration "advises" pilots to stay a minimum of 2,000 feet above parks and designated wilderness areas, but legions of pilots dismiss that stricture as purely advisory, without force. In 1986 a plane and a helicopter elbowed each other for viewing room over the Grand Canyon. When a helicopter elbow collides with a fixed-wing's straight-arm, the results are eventful for both: 24 tourists gawked for the last time that day.

We wish the list of offenders ended with the military, the bureaucracy, and couch-potato tourists. Alas, there's more bad news. Some of those who should be more vigilant in defending wilderness values seem to be losing their vigilance when it comes to bringing aircraft in over wild backcountry.

Backcountry skiers value the peace and serenity of the quiet snow-laden hills—or at least some do. Others pay to get there quick via helicopter. Helicopter skiing is an increasingly popular sport for the affluent, and an increasing intrusion on the peace and serenity the other skiers went out there to find. Writes one skier in Utah's Wasatch Range:

> I go out into the backcountry here to enjoy the solitude, peace, and beauty (and, yes, even untracked powder).... I will be in a wonderful space, physically and mentally, and then "chop…chop…chop…" the intrusion of a helicopter blasts that all away. Whether listening to it, or actually having it land nearby, the atmosphere is altered. Suddenly it feels like a competitive race, a selfish feeling grows, and it seems impossible to get back into the graceful movement of the day.

Within the past few years two of New England's most venerable hiking clubs have celebrated anniversaries of the construction of historic backcountry hostels up in the mountains. In both instances these clubs proposed to fly guests and supplies up to the hostels for the celebrations. Only the voiced disapproval of White Mountain National Forest officials prevented the mountains from being subjected to the intermittent drone of helicopters flying in and out over the wilderness. We applaud the stand of the forest officials and very much regret that the leadership of those two clubs did not see the point without having to be chided. We thought conservation organizations were supposed to oversee government agencies on preserving wilderness, not vice versa.

Obviously some people seem to think a helicopter is just a helpful tool to be employed whenever useful. That certainly is one point of view. But anyone with a respect for wilderness values knows otherwise. Like the radio, the helicopter is a tie to our civilized world, intruding into our efforts to become a part of a natural world. Those who casually bring the radio or the helicopter to the backcountry are making those two worlds more alike. It absolutely must be the objective of wilderness management to keep these worlds separate and distinct.

In the White Mountains helicopters were once a rare sight. During the 1960s Justice William O. Douglas wrote a well-publicized article on the famed huts in the White Mountains and asked one of the hut boys working there, Wouldn't it be easier to bring food and supplies in by helicopter instead of packing such heavy loads? "Not on your life!" was the response: "Then the romance would go out of the huts. Backpacking brings a sense of achievement." Justice Douglas agreed. But within a couple of years of that exchange, other heads in the hut system management came to a new view of the matter. When a new hut was built in 1964, construction materials were largely flown to the mountain site, and soon thereafter helicopters were in regular use supplying all of the huts in the system, typically with three fly-ins per season. The hut crew continues to backpack up many day-to-day supplies, but the much larger crowds now enjoying the huts could not be accommodated without those large fly-ins three times per summer.

What has happened since 1964 is an unfolding saga that reveals the risks of letting a camel's nose into the tent.

During the 1970s there was an accident at lovely Carter Notch, a secluded spot in the White Mountains. The victim had to be carried down 3.8 miles of mountain trail at night. Soon thereafter a committee of the Appalachian Mountain Club proposed a plan for going into a wild and picturesque boulder field in Carter Notch, moving the boulders around, adding a bit of concrete, and creating a helicopter landing pad there. The plan would make helicopter rescue possible for future accidents, and in the process provide a better way for supplying AMC's nearby Carter Notch Hut. The plan became a highly controversial point of debate and was soon brought up for reconsideration. The pro-pad forces were led, naturally enough, by the helicopter pilot who would most often use the proposed pad (and whose company would of course be paid for the flights). The anti-pad forces elicited a response from the scientific community, including botanists who feared for the impact on a certain rare plant that grew only in that boulder field. ("Your snail darter," sneered the pro-pad forces.) In addition the White Mountain National Forest pointed out to the committee that AMC did not have the authority to go knocking over boulders or otherwise rearranging a national forest to suit its convenience, and that the plan would have to be approved by the forest supervisor and be accompanied by an environmental impact statement, with opportunity for public comment. One of your authors was a member of this AMC committee at the time and recalls the day of the meeting at which the plan was to be finally debated and voted on. We sat there eyeing our fellow committee members and trying to figure out how the vote would go, and thought it might be close. Fortunately (for the boulders) the debate displayed the folly of the plan and the vote was 11–1 to reject it.

Still, for many years the AMC supplied another of its huts by helicopter flights directly over the Great Gulf Wilderness, openly flouting the federal advisory regulation. Its helicopter pilot often flew friends up to huts just for the fun of it, and finally that pilot landed a boat and camping supplies in a remote pond in a designated wilderness area. That last caper was a direct violation of the law, a formal investigation and hearing ensued, the pilot was fined, and the White Mountain National Forest initiated a more stringent program of controls on aircraft activity over the forest by anyone—but with special relevance to the hitherto-casual excesses of the AMC.

The problem is nationwide. A recent survey reported in the *New York Times* disclosed that no fewer than 90 national parks and monuments, one-fourth of the total, cite problems with inappropriate aircraft activity. As a result, the US Forest Service and the National Park Service have conducted a joint study of the problem. As we go to press with this book the results of that study are expected soon.

In fairness, we should point out that the helicopter has played a useful role in the backcountry, one that even the most zealous proponents of wilderness values would have to acknowledge. Search and rescue comes to mind immediately. We have nothing but admiration for the courage and skill of helicopter pilots who fly rescue missions in the treacherous air currents of mountain terrain, often in highly unstable weather. One of the best, the boldest and most skillful is the same pilot we were talking about a moment ago.

One winter one of us was involved with finding and evacuating a pair of cold and helpless hikers marooned on a high forested ridge not far from tiny Garfield Pond. The weather was anything but pleasant that day, with snow-laden clouds swirling around the nearby craggy summit of Mount Garfield. After we got the victims to the pond, a Special Forces military helicopter swooped in, appeared out of the clouds, landed on the ice of the pond, took us all aboard, then veered off around the summit cone through the clouds and out over the valley to the nearest hospital. We were suitably impressed, and the victims were lucky to get out so quickly.

Nor is search and rescue the only legitimate activity of helicopters in the backcountry. One of the problems generated by the backpacking boom was a tremendous load of human wastes at popular camping sites in remote locations. It was far too much for traditional pit privies to handle in vulnerable sites with shallow soils and threatened groundwater. Among the solutions found for this problem, one has been to place 55-gallon drums under the outhouse seats, close them (tight!) when full, winch them out of the outhouse, then have the helicopter whisk them off to a suitable disposal site in the valley.

Yet another useful service of the helicopter in the backcountry has been in supplying the Appalachian Mountain Club huts in the White Mountains. That's not quite such a clear-cut gain. AMC officials will argue a persuasive case that the huts cannot function without air supply. That's undoubtedly true, given the present methods of operation of the huts. The problem comes in resisting the temptation to indulge in overuse of helicopters, to

fly those champagne glasses up to the hut for a party, to fly club
dignitaries or special guests in on occasion. While the National
Forest officials do their best to control such excesses, the only
effective answer is for the responsible officials of AMC to look
more closely at what's at stake here. If club leaders feel deeply
enough about preserving the sanctity of the backcountry, they'll
police themselves well. What is needed is a recognition that the
sound of a helicopter is an offensive intrusion on the wilderness
experience of just about everyone who's out there, a necessary evil
to be employed only when truly necessary and appropriate. With a
sympathetic reflection on that point, AMC will surely come
around to reducing and controlling the use of aircraft in the
backcountry.

Bill McKibben, writing of the presence of power boats on a
quiet pond, has expressed the message well:

> It is not so much the danger—few swimmers, I imagine, ever
> die by Evinrude. It's not even so much the blue smoke that
> hangs low over the water. It's that the motorboat gets in your
> mind. You're forced to think, not feel—to think of human
> society and people. The lake is utterly different on these days,
> just as the planet is utterly different now.

Thus does the presence of aircraft over the backcountry alter
that world. It flies into your mind as well as over your body, and
that is an even more unpardonable intrusion.

"The interesting puzzle in our time," observes Langdon
Winner in *The Whale and the Reactor*, "is that we so willingly
sleepwalk through the process of reconstituting the conditions of
human existence." With casual overuse of aircraft, we sleepwalk
into a basic alteration of the backcountry experience for everyone
who's out there.

This is another reason why it is so vital, as we have been
arguing, that we move on from thinking of wilderness in purely
physical terms, in terms only of protecting the physical resource.
We need to take the next step. Just as important as physical
conservation is the spiritual experience—the spirit of wildness, of a

sense of remoteness from the bustle and technology of civilization, of solitude and stillness, of adventure and genuine risk, of a closeness to the natural world and a distance from the civilized world, a sense of being in a realm where people are passing visitors and not significant agents of change.

If we look on wilderness in purely physical terms, we may tolerate a lot of activities therein that become less appropriate if we take the larger view of wilderness as an experience, embracing also our minds, our spirits.

Case Study

A Night in Odell's Gully

There were giants in the earth in those days.

GENESIS 6:4

MARCH 24, 1968, 2:55 P.M. of a Sunday afternoon. A howling storm raged over Mount Washington, the Northeast's highest peak. One of the country's top ice climbers of that day, Ed Nester, was having a bowl of soup with his fiancée in the Pinkham Notch lodge at the base of Washington. They had climbed the ice on the mountain on Saturday, but the deteriorating weather that morning had led them to decide to stay off the ice, dry out, and prepare to go home. As soon as they finished their soup, they'd start the long drive back to New York City.

They never finished that bowl of soup.

The telephone that connected Pinkham with a string of emergency lines up on the mountain rang. A young woman answered, then ran out the door, then back in again. Nester asked her if anything had happened, hoping the answer would be reassuring. She asked him to speak to the Forest Service ranger on the telephone.

High up in Huntington Ravine, that steep-sided glacial cirque whose ice-choked gullies attract ice climbers from all over the East, two ice climbers were stranded, unable to get down. While climbing in the bad weather, they had been hit by an avalanche. A third member of their party, carried lower by the avalanche, had managed to get down and send word for help.

The ranger told Nester that the two were OK, but unable to get down on their own. Could Nester come up and lead a rescue? Nester thought to himself, "If they are OK and the weather is so bad that they can't get down, how am I going to get up to them?" But he agreed to start up.

Up on the mountain, things had already started to happen. Just below the floor of Huntington Ravine is a cabin used as a base by ice climbers. It was to this cabin that the shaken climber, Donn Stahlman, had made it down with the news about his stranded partners, Jeff Damp and Tom Davis. At the cabin he found another climber, Charlie Porter, who used an emergency phone to notify the Forest Service rangers, then returned to the cabin and prepared to start up himself.

Porter and Stahlman left the cabin and began trudging up through the storm toward the floor of Huntington Ravine. In minutes they were overtaken by a huge Thiokol snow machine, which took them on board and continued slowly crunching up toward the base of the ice gullies above. Also aboard were two Forest Service rangers and two employees of the Appalachian Mountain Club, which maintains the lodge down at Pinkham Notch.

By 3:20 the six men stood in the floor of Huntington Ravine. Above them towered the rocky walls of the mountain, through which several gullies wend upward, filled with deep snow for the most part, but with hard blue water ice at the steepest points. One of these gullies is known as Odell's (after the first man to climb it). On that particular Sunday afternoon, however, none of the gullies nor any other feature could be distinguished from below. A swirling, howling storm of snow and high winds reduced visibility to a few feet. The temperature hovered at about 0°F, winds gusting to

75 miles per hour, according to actual observations made at the Summit Observatory, some 2,000 feet further up the mountain.

From their knowledge of the Huntington terrain, the six men were able to work their way up through the storm to where the snow steepened into ice at the bottom of Odell's Gully. They shouted up into the maelstrom above, but their voices were swallowed insignificantly in the shriek of the storm. Was it possible that two men were up there somewhere, still alive after sitting motionless on a precarious icy ledge for two and a half hours?

Porter and Stahlman roped up, and Porter began to lead up the ice. After one rope's length, he tied himself in and signaled for Stahlman to follow. As he climbed, Stahlman found that one ankle was weakened from the strains of his tumble in the avalanche earlier that day. He was barely able to reach the stance that Porter had chopped out on the ice slope above. As soon as he did, Porter was off again, working his way to the right edge of the gully and eventually to a niche in the side of the cliff there, which the climbers came to call "the cave."

At this point, however, Stahlman was simply unable to climb further. Exhausted, injured, cold, and buffeted by the relentless winds and blowing ice crystals that froze on the climbers' eyelashes, tending to freeze the eyelids shut, Stahlman retreated. He descended one of their ropes to the base of the ice, where one of the Forest Service rangers escorted him down to the more sheltered floor of the ravine and eventually on down to the cabin. One of the AMC employees had already descended too.

That left one ranger and one AMC man up at the base of the ice; Charlie Porter two pitches up at the "cave"; and somewhere up above there in the storm, the stranded pair, Damp and Davis. The time was 4:25. Not much daylight left.

Porter shouted up into the wind once more and this time a faint human sound echoed back. He shouted again. Answering shouts responded through a lull in the snowy inferno. Damp and Davis were alive—and from what he could gather, Porter understood them to be not seriously injured. It was clear, however, that their condition must be deteriorating, immobilized as long as they were, without shelter on a small ledge up there on the steep ice, exposed to the full force of the storm. Porter shouted down to the two men at the base of the ice. By this time, though, with steeper ice above him, and very cold and tired himself from his prolonged struggle against the storm, Porter could go no further. He rigged the ropes carefully to prepare to descend.

Meanwhile, down at Pinkham Notch, Ed Nester had gathered his equipment together and was soon aboard a second snow machine, being driven up the mountain. Somewhere near the cabin that machine broke down and Nester continued on foot. He met two climbers coming down and asked if they knew how to do technical ice climbing. One of them said he did. "How technical?" asked Nester. "Very technical," replied the other, who turned out to be Dave Seidman, who had just the previous summer made the first ascent of the South Face of Mount McKinley, a daring climb that stamped him as one of the top up-and-coming mountaineers of this country. Seidman willingly agreed to join Nester.

It is difficult to say what might have been the outcome of the story had it not been for this fortuitous linking-up, on a late Sunday afternoon, of two outstanding ice climbers, Nester and Seidman. Both were to play key roles in the events of the next 12 hours.

About 5:30 Nester and Seidman reached the base of the ice. The storm was now at its height, darkness nearly complete. The peak gust of wind officially recorded that evening on the summit was 104 miles per hour. The temperature dropped to −2°F. When the rescue pair arrived, the remaining forest ranger, close to the edge of survival himself, immediately descended.

Nester asked Seidman if he wanted to lead. Seidman said the idea didn't overly excite him. Nester asked again, and Seidman agreed to give it a try.

The two pitches up to the cave, where Porter still huddled by himself, went fairly smoothly, despite the worsening storm. The three men exchanged information, and Porter then finally descended the fixed and partly frozen ropes. He and eventually everyone else in the ravine retreated to the warmth and security of the cabin below.

Up at the cave, Seidman prepared to lead the steep ice above to try and reach the stranded climbers. The storm was now so bad that nothing could be heard above the wind from up there. Seidman shouted to Nester: "It looks hard—I'll mostly likely fall." Then he swung his ice ax and began to climb.

It was 8:00 P.M. before Seidman, calling on all the resources of a superb ice leader, reached the ledge where Damp and Davis hunched motionless. Working as quickly as the wind and cold permitted, Seidman rigged solid anchors in the ice and lowered the two climbers to the cave, then descended himself.

In the process of lowering Damp, the full extent of their predicament became clear for the first time: during the afternoon avalanche, one of Damp's crampons had stabbed into his leg, leaving a serious wound and resulting in much loss of blood. He could not put any weight on the injured leg, and wounds of that severity have a tendency to weaken the body's defenses against cold and wind chill. The lowering over the steep pitch above the cave was possible precisely because it was steep—Seidman could simply let Damp down like a sack of frozen potatoes. Below, where the angle was less, would not be so easy.

Nevertheless, Seidman and Nester felt they had reason for optimism now that the actual rescue had begun. They were all down at the cave now. All that remained was to descend to the base of the ice and arrange for Damp to be littered down the steep snow below, to where a snow machine could take him out.

Seidman went down first, to clear the frozen ropes. When he reached the base of the ice, confident that the others would soon be down, and totally exhausted himself, he immediately set off down through the storm. It was 9:00 when he reached the cabin, told the assembled rescue teams that the others were on their way down but would need a litter for Damp from the base of the ice, and collapsed for some badly needed and richly deserved rest. Through those early evening hours he had absorbed the maximum strain of leading difficult ice in the dark at the height of the storm, lowering the stranded pair, then clearing the frozen ropes below.

The rescue team set off from the cabin and fought their way back up in the dark and storm, hauling a toboggan-type litter. It took until 10:30 before four of them reached the base of the ice.

To their consternation the only person there was Davis, helpless from exhaustion and cold and unable to explain where Nester and Damp might be. The rescuers got Davis up and escorted him down to the cabin. They radioed to Pinkham Notch that more technical help was needed to get to Nester and Damp.

After Seidman had left the cave, Nester had tried to lower Davis. Because of the angle of descent, however, this had not worked. Somehow Davis got back up to the cave, and Nester then rigged him up for a rappel of the frozen ropes. After over an hour Davis finally reached the base of the ice.

The ropes above him froze solidly to the slope, however, and Nester was unable to determine whether Davis was in fact off the ropes yet or not. Furthermore, all the available ropes were now thoroughly frozen and useless for lowering Damp—and in any case the strategy had not worked for lowering the able-bodied Davis, so it clearly would be both futile and dangerous to attempt to lower the injured Damp single-handedly. Left to handle the situation by himself, with no one around to get up to him, and unable to see or hear anything of what was going on at the base of the ice, Nester evaluated his predicament. He knew that he could descend the ropes himself and find out what the problem was at the base of the ice—even perhaps, if help were there, instruct them on how to control the descent of Damp if he could get another rope to lower him with. However, if he went down he could by no means be sure of getting back up. And if he didn't get back up, Damp would surely die.

Nester decided to prepare to last the night on the wind-racked ice ledge. He tried wrapping a lightweight rescue blanket around Damp. The wind first frustrated his efforts, then eventually tore the blanket to shreds. He cut off Damp's crampons and somehow stuffed the injured climber into a bivouac bag just big enough for one person. He then shoved him into the corner of the ice wall and lay against him to protect him further from the wind.

He talked to Damp all during the night, asking him questions about school, climbing, anything to keep his consciousness engaged. In the late hours, Damp haltingly asked if he were going to make it through the night or whether he would die. Nester told him, by God, he'd better make it; what was the point of wasting this night up here for nothing?

The scene at the cave through that long night exceeds the imagination of anyone who has not seen a mountain storm in full fury.

There is a limit beyond which the human body cannot endure cold and exhaustion. When a person nears that limit, the mind will accept any rationalization to justify its own survival instinct and defend a decision to get to safety. In light of this, it is singular that Nester—having thought through the logic of descending the frozen ropes himself to see what was the matter below, but having also realized that if he did not get back up, Damp would die—having that rationalization full in front of him, nevertheless determined to stay up there in that storm and risk his own life, not just in a single moment, but through a long punishing night, to save the life of a climber he'd never met before.

If there has been a clearer example of sheer personal heroism, we've never heard of it.

Dimly aware of the precarious predicament of the stranded pair, rescuers who brought back Davis had called for additional technical support. Charlie Porter, who had been sleeping soundly after his own great efforts earlier that day, was roused. Another climber was located at Pinkham. It was 1:00 in the morning before the two were taken up the mountain in the snow machine. Once in the darkened, stormswept ravine, they found that all trace of tracks had been blown away. This resulted in their heading up first into the wrong gully. By the time they reached the base of the ice in Odell's, it was 4:00 A.M.

Now, finally, the storm had begun to abate. With the wind less noisy, their loud calls were heard and answered by Nester. Incredibly, Nester and Damp were still alive up there. Porter and the other climber, George Smith, began the ascent. Beginning daylight soon assisted their labors. They rigged a well-anchored system for lowering Nester and Damp on the same rope, Nester guiding the helpless injured man's descent. At the base of the ice a further handicap was added when overeager support rescuers let the toboggan-litter get away from them, to slide uselessly 1,000 feet down the mountain empty. Nester set up a brake-bar system using his ice ax, then lowered Damp's recumbent form down the long snow slope, supported on either side by other rescuers. Eventually they got down to where the snow machine could pick up the victim and take him down the long mountain trail to a waiting ambulance.

Above, Porter and Smith retrieved ropes and gear and lingered to watch the dawn of a lovely day. "In fact," recalled Smith, "this was the best winter morning I had ever seen."

That Damp and his friends recovered completely from the night in Odell's Gully was nothing short of a miracle—a miracle with names like Ed Nester, Dave Seidman, and Charlie Porter. The mountain gods, having shrieked so pitilessly all night, in the end relented.

But the mountain gods are fickle. They respect no heroes. Scarcely more than a year later, an enormous avalanche rushed blindly down Dhaulagiri, halfway round the world in the Himalayas, and buried seven men, among them Dave Seidman. A few summers after that, during a descent from a difficult route in the Canadian Rockies, a rappel anchor pulled loose and sent another climber to his death on the glacier below—Ed Nester.

Those two names, however, will always be associated in honor for what they did a quarter century ago, on a night in Odell's Gully.

A detailed hour-by-hour account of this incident, told by some of those involved, was published in Appalachia, *journal of the Appalachian Mountain Club, in December 1968.*

14

The High Cost of Search and Rescue

Of course there's danger; but a certain amount of danger
is essential to the quality of life. I don't believe in taking
foolish chances; but nothing can be accomplished without
taking any chance at all.
I believe the risks I take are justified by the sheer love of the
life I lead. Yes, just being in the air on a flight across the
ocean to Paris, warrants the hazard of an ice field below.

CHARLES LINDBERGH, *THE SPIRIT OF ST. LOUIS*

THE HEROES OF Odell Gully performed their work as part of a relatively small group of volunteer rescuers. But that was a quarter century ago. Now search and rescue is big business. It's a growth industry, running amok in the garden of the backcountry. The consequences for the spirit of wildness need to be considered.

Every year some people underestimate the ruggedness of the backcountry and wind up being hauled out from their mountain idyll by rescuers. The lucky ones are those that live to profit by the experience. Meanwhile, the mounting cost and human effort devoted to mountain rescue is beginning to attract ominous public concern. Let's relate an example.

The Edmands Col Special

In 1975, on April Fool's Day—that date may be significant—two young hikers started out to climb in the White Mountains' Presidential Range.

Now, there are those who believe that T. S. Eliot may have done some late-winter climbing in the Presidentials to have come to the conclusion that April is the cruelest month. It is a time when southern New England is beginning to glow with spring's first bloom—but the snow and cold still lie thick up on the northern slopes. Winter lurks in wait for the unwary.

These two young hikers wore summer-weight hiking boots and no snowshoes. They reached a tiny shelter that the Forest Service maintained for emergency use only at the high pass between mounts Adams and Jefferson, the second- and third-highest peaks in the Northeast. This pass is called Edmands Col. They intended to continue early the next morning.

In fact, the two were not to leave Edmands Col for seven long cold days and night.

Screaming winds, biting cold, and the biggest snowfall of that winter piled into those inhospitable mountains. Soon state officials, Forest Service rangers, and the experienced personnel of the Appalachian Mountain Club were combing the snow-covered hills, fighting the arctic conditions, trying to locate the missing pair. It was a grueling effort, but unlike many such rescue efforts, which all too often arrive too late, this one succeeded in finding and evacuating the stranded hikers with no one seriously hurt.

When the monumental rescue effort was over and all were safely down, people began to think about what had happened. A tremendous number of rescuers had exposed themselves to arduous work and even personal danger. The total cost was estimated as approaching $10,000. AMC's mountain-wise staff alone contributed more than 600 person-hours. The state's Fish and Game Department had tied up many rangers for days. So had the US Forest Service.

People began not only to think but also to emote. Some of them began to sound off with some highly emotional conclusions:

Many local hunters and fishermen, well aware that hunting and fishing licenses pay the freight for Fish and Game Department work, began to scream about where that money was going.

Newspaper editorials, including one in the influential *Manchester Union Leader*, proposed that hikers and climbers be licensed before being allowed into the hills, the fees going to support search-and-rescue efforts.

AMC official Robert Proudman in *Appalachia* warned: "If many more rescues like this one develop... someday the hiker may find that laws have been legislated to control his activities and to develop revenue for the inevitable rescues that arise from the pursuit of hiking and mountaineering sports."

Some voices urged an end to all mountain rescues. "It seems to me that the moral obligation of being 'thy brother's keeper' ends at that point where brother knowingly and willingly places himself in the way of danger," cried one letter-to-the-editor writer in *Appalachia*. To such people, the answer to more hikers in distress was simple: Do nothing. Force them to take care of themselves or accept the consequences.

Less than a year after that April Fools' incident, three of us were getting ready to go on a winter climbing venture in the same general area when we stopped for gas at a station near the trailhead. We ran into a torrent of outrage expressed by the local proprietor, condemning anyone who went into the hills in winter, and loudly articulating the sportsman's complaint that he didn't want his license fee money used to rescue idiots up there. "Let 'em freeze," he cried.

"There Oughtta Be a Law!"

That 1975 experience is repeated in various forms every few years and in different mountain ranges all over the country. Seven years later in the same Presidential Range, two ice climbers stupidly got lost on Mount Washington. During a massive search for them, one of the would-be rescuers, a popular youth named Albert Dow, was himself swept under by an avalanche. Dow's death became a symbol to many angry people of how the reckless and thoughtless acts of climbers can jeopardize the very lives of rescuers, let alone thousands of dollars of public and private expense.

Seven years after that—there's a pattern here, isn't there?— two separate incidents found summertime climbers lost, one a few miles north, the other a few miles west of the Presidentials. Search parties started to hunt, at first tentatively, but gradually mounting in scope, intensity, and the numbers of rescuers involved. Large detachments from state agencies, the US Forest Service, and the Appalachian Mountain Club were joined by legions of woodswise volunteers, local rescue service personnel, and military units. Though one of the search locales included a federally designated wilderness area, rescuers did not hesitate to send in all-terrain vehicles in large numbers. Publicity commanded front-page space in local papers and up-to-the-minute radio and television coverage. After days of beating the bushes (literally!), rescuers found the bodies, much too late in both cases. Indeed, one of the lost pair had deliberately gone out to end his life in the woods.

Not surprisingly, these incidents lead to cries for legislation or some form of restraint on the freedom of the hills. Rescue personnel see vividly the risks to which backcountry recreationists expose themselves. Local citizens and taxpayers see the frightful cost of rescues. Fifteen years ago an official of the Mountain Rescue Association estimated the cost of a typical mountain rescue at more than $25,000. Considering the rampant inflation since then, together with the development of expensive new search-and-rescue technology, we shudder to think what the cost must run these days.

In states where backcountry rescues occur all too frequently, the legislatures have entertained several possible laws to deal with the problem:

- Billing victims for rescue costs
- Mandating that each hiker purchase a "hiker's license" before entering mountain trails
- Slapping an excise tax on hiking equipment, the proceeds going to a rescue fund
- Requiring each hiker to carry an electronic device that will signal his location if lost

One has to be sympathetic with public anger about the enormous costs expended in efforts to save people who often have acted foolishly. That such people should pay the costs of rescue efforts seems to us an unarguable point. If you get yourself in trouble, you get yourself out, or you pay. But the simplicity of that reasoning is deceptive. Do we really mean that if an impoverished college student makes a mistake, and one of those $100,000 rescue efforts goes into saving him, that dope should be saddled with debts for the rest of his life to pay it all back? Still, that's a quibble. We entirely support the proposition that if you get in trouble in the mountains, you are accountable for the time and effort of others who come in to get you.

When proposals move on from there, reasonable voices may be heard urging caution and warning about the potential impact on the freedom of the hills.

Some skeptics have asked what would happen if state officials pushed the rescue button for hikers or climbers who felt that they had their situation under control and could get themselves out. This has happened. Suppose the state and cooperating agencies put in considerable time and cost looking for a party of overdue hikers, but the hikers themselves felt they could have walked out on their own eventually. Would they have to pay?

We were with a party of highly experienced winter climbers on Katahdin one December. One of our people, walking in to our rendezvous point, decided to bivouac overnight along the trail. Baxter State Park management knew our plans, so when he didn't arrive at the rendezvous that night, park officials zoomed out in their snowmobiles looking for him, woke us up to send us on a futile, middle-of-the-night search of the mountain's trails, and alerted all park personnel, along with the state police, to be ready for full-scale search operations. The next morning our friend strolled up to our camp, blissfully unaware of all the excitement. Under some of the ill-conceived legislative proposals he could have been billed for quite a hunk of change.

A very real practical problem with the proposed hiking license is that hikers who purchase the license may feel that they are thereby guaranteed cost-free rescue services. AMC's spokesman at New Hampshire legislative hearings on one bill expressed concern that such a license could lead to more rescues:

> We are rather sure that we will be going up into the hills quite regularly to bring out tired hikers who have realized that rescue service is now available to them for only the cost of their "license." It seems that six or eight dollars is pretty cheap for a helicopter or litter ride out of the mountains anywhere, anytime.

A long-experienced climber we know, Robert Kruszyna, has set forth an interesting and well-conceived argument that rescue activity should be greatly reduced from current levels. He argues that lost or injured hikers are not, in the strict sense, "innocent" victims:

> They have chosen of their own free will to be there and to engage in whatever risky activity they are doing.... It is a simple matter of free choice and responsibility. Personally, I view the prospect of a guaranteed search and rescue as robbing climbing of its sense of adventure, which is probably the only meaningful justification for an otherwise useless activity. Risk is an intrinsic part of that sense of adventure. Those who seek out the wild country must accept it and its consequences.

Kruszyna has been unfairly accused of a posture of "Let them die." That is not his position. What he *is* proposing is restraint. There are situations where rescue personnel should wait a while before starting action. If someone is late, maybe one night out in the woods or on the cliff would not be too bad—at least not worth the mobilizing of dozens of rescuers and expensive procedures. In wilderness areas, spare the use of motorized equipment. Take it easy, everyone. Kruszyna reports:

> I have personally observed a case where a search was initiated in a fit of zeal while the purported victims were calmly and competently extricating themselves from their difficulty, which was simply that their climb took longer than they anticipated. There are too many quick whistles in this game.

One especially important point to note is the perverse effect of rescue activity: well-publicized rescue capability generates its own business. The more we signal to hikers and climbers that rescue capability is standing by to help them if they get in trouble, the more we invite hikers and climbers to extend themselves into risky situations, secure in the conviction that someone will bail them out. Sensational press coverage of accidents and rescues encourages public thinking that rescues are routinely available.

There is no question that this perverse effect already is felt. After one rescue at Garfield Pond, one of the rescued victims was overheard explaining that he felt no remorse about having to be rescued because that was what all those folks were paid to do. (We never got *our* check!) We have heard of numerous incidents where climbers have continued up in the face of deteriorating weather or hikers have sat down and waited for rescuers, precisely because they confidently expect the massive search-and-rescue apparatus to be mobilized on their behalf. A special survey by the Society for American Foresters found in 1989 that

> Wilderness managers report that requests for search-and-rescue assistance have increased, and often for less serious injuries than in the past.

The prestigious American Alpine Club has criticized National Park Service efforts to make parks ultrasafe as "admirable for the urbanized areas of the parks, but is it what we need in the backcountry?"

Backpacker magazine, one spokesman for the pedestrian outdoorsperson, in an editorial suggested, "Let's sign waivers letting the government off the hook for our safety in the backcountry."

Mount Everest climber Willi Unsoeld argued that no one has the obligation to search for "lost" climbers. He contended: "No government agency, especially, has any obligation to save the lives of stupid citizens who take foolhardy risks." Unsoeld was emphatically opposed to the all-for-safety theory of what a climber should undertake. The fact that Unsoeld himself lost his life in an avalanche only adds credibility to his credo.

This philosophy was summed up in its most stirring form by the gallant Antarctic explorer Captain Robert Scott, dying alone with his comrades in the frozen wastes, who wrote in his diary: "We took risks, we know we took them. Things have come out against us; therefore we have no cause for complaint."

Too Much Rescue?

One underlying problem that these issues mask is the question of whether we aren't, all of us collectively, becoming too rescue-happy. When people go into the backcountry, they implicitly accept (or certainly ought to accept) some level of risk. If you want to be 100 percent sure of safety, take up checkers or bridge or bowling, not hiking or climbing. If a hiker doesn't return from his hike, we should probably go to look for him, yes. But how many of us? And at what level of cost to the taxpayer?

As things stand now, a typical scenario can go like this. Three hikers set out to climb Mount Washington in November. Two turn back because the weather above treeline is foul. The third continues and finds his trip taking a long time. As darkness approaches, his two friends report him missing. A series of radio calls goes out to the various manned backcountry facilities on the mountain—the Mount Washington Observatory, the Appalachian Mountain Club shelter in Tuckerman Ravine, the Harvard Mountaineering Club cabin in Huntington Ravine, the Randolph Mountain Club lodge in the Northern Presidentials. The snow rangers of the US Forest Service are notified. New Hampshire Fish and Game officials are advised. Expert climbers from Mountain Rescue Service are alerted. As darkness descends forces are mobilized and search parties begin to comb the mountain. A nearby military unit is asked to participate and sends in a helicopter, which flies over the above-treeline terrain in the fading light. There is a heady feeling to all this activity. Rescue parties feel a mounting sense of excitement. Everyone hopes he'll be the one to find the victim. We know some local folk who keep a radio tuned in to hear about such incidents and who will leap into their rescue gear to go join the fray at any hour of day or night. A mood evolves wherein no stone shall be left unturned, no expense spared. Tense voices fill the airwaves with dramatic phrases like "Unit 17 this is Unit 20, Unit 17 this is Unit 20" or "Do you copy" or "Stand by" or (our favorite) "Ten Four." (Don't ask us why "Ten Four" is easier to say than "OK," but it sounds a lot more exciting over the radio.)

Sometime during the evening the missing hiker wanders in. Having found the way up icy and treacherous, he elected to walk down the auto road and back the long way around. He is amazed to learn anyone was looking for him. On their sides, the rescuers heap scorn and outrage on the poor sap, for having cost everyone all this trouble and expense.

Why don't we think about this a little bit? When a hiker is reported missing, sure, let's check around by radio and see if anyone has seen him. Maybe one or two people might wander up the more likely routes of descent. But dozens of people? A helicopter? Government agencies and crack teams of mountain rescuers? Do we really need to mobilize the entire eclectic army of rescue capability at each call of alarm?

A local newspaper reported on May 3, 1991:

> More than 150 rescue workers, a helicopter and a police dog searched the Appalachian Trail for 13 hours Saturday and yesterday for a hiker who was late for dinner but said he was never lost.

> The massive search ended at 11:15 A.M. yesterday,
> when two volunteer firemen discovered David Evans,
> 30, walking home on Jug End Road.

This sort of overreaction seems to be a growing malady. A little common sense, calmness, and willingness to forego opportunities for personal heroism may be appropriate.

A situation developed in the Adirondacks for a while under which the rescue function of rangers became the chief rationale for maintaining budget levels in the state agency. So the agency began to document every single hour spent on rescue work; rescue opportunities were alertly spotted: public letter-writing campaigns were stimulated, focused on the value of rescue programs; and the real bread-and-butter duties of trail maintenance, fire control, public information, and environmental protection were given a back seat. As one observer of this situation concluded:

> In the end, most of the ranger positions were salvaged, but in the process some implicit promises were made to the hiking public: that rangers exist for no other purpose than to help lost or injured hikers, and that backcountry rescue was now another of the many entitlements due each citizen.

We came perilously close to a quantum leap in the wrong direction through litigation recently. In June 1987 hikers in Grand Teton National Park became lost descending 11,938-foot Buck Mountain; one died of hypothermia. A lawsuit was launched, claiming that park officials didn't institute rescue quickly enough. The plaintiff argued that park officials have an obligation to require safety equipment, to test the competency of each climber, and to "clear" the mountains of all climbers before dark. The park properly balked. Superintendent Stark argued that they hadn't the manpower or funds to carry out such functions, but perhaps more important: "The inherent dangers of mountain climbing are patently obvious;" and "many Park visitors value backcountry climbing as one of the few experiences free from government regulation or interference."

Three cheers for Superintendent Stark! And three more for the court which upheld him. Had the plaintiff won, who knows what obligations would have been imposed by law on every national park and forest agency, and by extension, on every state and private agency with rescue responsibilities. Fortunately the U.S. 10th Circuit Court of Appeals in Denver ruled that rescues are discretionary. According to columnist Penelope Purdy, this was "the best possible ruling that backcountry lovers could have wanted." Attorney, climber, and past president of the American Alpine Club, James P. McCarthy, has called this decision "the most important court decision involving backcountry use in recent memory." Had it gone the other way, both Purdy and McCarthy suspect the federal government might have had to close parks and forests to recreationists rather than deal with the absurd obligation (and cost!) which an adverse ruling would have implied.

Yet there seem to be rescue groups who almost want to push in precisely this direction: hop out and start looking at the first sign of trouble. Send that signal to everyone that rescue is something we do here. That's the wrong message to be sending to backcountry recreationists. Adirondack hiker-climber, Tony Goodwin, himself long experienced in rescue work and gravely concerned that it's all getting out of hand, has warned:

> Now that the rescue genie is out of the bottle, getting back to the days of providing less service will not be easy. Perhaps the best that we can hope for is that the "more is better" mentality will cease before we end up with a backcountry version of a full-service city fire department.

Well, if you spill a bag of granola in the chicken yard, it's hard to pick it up. It won't be easy to reverse the direction in which the philosophy and practice of search and rescue has been heading in recent years. But if we care enough about preserving the spirit of wildness, this is an issue that needs to be addressed. There are encouraging signs that responsible and conservative organizations are prepared to show leadership in this area. The Society of American Forests has proposed:

Wilderness visitors should confront the wilderness on its own terms. It is the visitors' responsibility to ensure that they have the skills to travel and camp safely in the backcountry.

Like many of the other issues we're raising in this book, a question of values is at stake here. So is our perception of what kind of backcountry we can and should have. What level of rescue effort is consistent with preserving the spirit of wildness?

IV

WHAT KIND OF BACKCOUNTRY DO WE WANT?

15

Of Time and Wildness

We all of us have been time-minded all our lives.
EUDORA WELTY, *ONE WRITER'S BEGINNING*

WE NEVER HAVE been able to keep a wristwatch. Hiking, camping in the mountains, rock climbing, ice climbing—these activities were never destined to suffer an exposed crystal on the forearm.

Years ago we repeatedly tried a variety of wristwatches. Weekend rock climbing kept the crystal so scratched and scuffed that you had to peer intently through the cobweb of scars to try to make out what the hands beneath might have to say. Glissading down a steep snow slope on Mount Clay in January brought one watch to its untimely (if you'll pardon the expression) demise, speared on the broken branch stub of a stunted spruce. It read 2:15. Presumably still does. A spectacular fall on an overhanging Shawangunk rock climb—caught by the rope, of course—ripped another timepiece from the wrist to a sudden end on a rocky ledge 40 feet below, at exactly 10:02 one morning.

Our local watch repairman came to know us well and fondly in those days. He appreciated our lavish patronage. Finally we awoke to how much of our money was moving across his counter into his cash register, and we stopped even trying to wear a wristwatch.

But in winter climbing, you need to know how many of those brief daylight hours you still have left. So we bought one of those cheap alarm clocks of the five-and-dime-store variety. To keep its works from freezing or getting discouraged in zero temperatures, we took to stuffing it in our shirt to keep it warm during the day, stowing it in the sleeping bag at night.

One morning we planned a big day climbing on Mount Washington. An early breakfast and predawn start was essential to our plans. We awoke the next morning to sunlight streaming in the tent, and a silent, stopped alarm clock. No big climb that day.

The obvious remedy for that predicament seemed to be to get *two* big dime-store alarm clocks, as insurance against one failing. Both stuffed in the shirt, of course.

This procedure began to give us a peculiar reputation. People would stop us to ask if we knew what time it was. Sure, we'd reply cheerfully, diving a hand into our shirt front and hauling out a large dime-store alarm clock—this in the middle of snow- and ice-chocked mountains in January, miles from the nearest road. When the questioner would get that incredulous stare on his face, we'd feel it necessary to check both clocks, and dive back into the shirt to produce the second. The inquirer would shuffle away, muttering, glancing nervously back over his shoulder.

Sometimes during a chat with a passing snowshoer in the woods, the conversation might momentarily cease, whereupon a startled look would cross the face of the traveler and he might ask, somewhat diffidently: "I say…are you ticking?"

About that time there were all those Cuban airplane-hijacking incidents and mad bombers smuggling their incendiary devices onto planes. People who ate lunch too close to us on a remote mountaintop would interrupt their sandwich in mid-chew to peer nervously in our direction when a lull in the wind gave the twin tickers a chance to be heard. The indisputable fact that no one had ever tried to hijack Mount Washington and take it to Havana seemed insufficient reassurance.

One day we led a difficult ice climb on Roaring Brook Falls in the Adirondacks. Perched atop the frozen first pitch, securely anchored to a boulder, we were belaying another ice climber up the crux move on the ice below. We had failed to notice that during our strenuous efforts on the climb, a button on our shirt had worked loose. Our friend, normally a cool and unflappable sort, was desperately clinging to his ice ax and clawing upward with his crampons, when the alarm clock whirred past him, inches from his ear, and plumped into the snow at the base of the ice. Our friend very nearly fell off.

Once, on a winter climb of Gothics' steep east face, our alarm clock saved the day. We and a friend had worked our way, adroitly we thought, through the worst defenses of the mountain, when the angle suddenly steepened and we wished we had put on the rope. In the silence of our concentration, as we carefully negotiated each precarious step, we began to get too nervous and tended to lean into the slope too much for safety. Suddenly, there on the frozen face, miles from any sign of human habitation, the alarm clock in our shirt went off. We managed to shut it off in about the time it takes a telephone to ring. Our friend turned around and dead-panned: "It's for you, Laura." We laughed, relaxed, and skipped across the steep section in good style, no longer tense or panicky.

After breaking almost as many dime-store alarm clocks as we did wristwatches before—now the lady in the dime store smiled warmly at our approach—we switched, first, to less flamboyant fold-up travel alarms, and finally to the very small and compact digital models.

Forget All Time?

Have you been wondering what all this rambling about clocks has to do with the subject of this book? Maybe we have digressed. But the issue of time is relevant to the spirit of the backcountry. Let's consider.

Many people heartily disapprove of this preoccupation with trying to keep time in the wilderness. There is a school of thought that argues you should get away from time when you go to the woods, that focus on the time of day is inconsistent with the spirit of wildness. In seeking a garden-of-Eden innocence in the wilderness, it is argued, we should, like Eve in *Paradise Lost*, "forget all time, all seasons, and their change, all please alike." We should go to the woods to be spontaneous and turn our backs on the time pressures and clock-watching of daily life.

As an ideal, an innocence of time is an appealing notion. But for a lot of practical reasons, we've never pursued that approach in the backwoods. There always seem to be many good reasons to know what time it is. How soon should we start making camp if we don't want to wash dishes in the dark? Have we got time to take that side trip over to the other summit? How can we be sure to get up early enough to be on the trail at first light, so we can be above treeline to watch the sun come up?

But heaven knows we don't want to turn into clock-watchers like *Alice in Wonderland*'s White Rabbit. Nor would we want to be overheard mumbling, like the White Rabbit, as we run down a mountain trail, "Oh my ears and whiskers, how late it's getting!" And we certainly wouldn't want to be seen, again like the famous rabbit, continually replacing our watch in our waistcoat pocket.

Nor would we want completely to lose track of time. No one would want to find themselves in the predicament of the March Hare and the Mad Hatter—where it's always six o'clock, teatime.

A Proper Sense of Time

We think that a due sense of time enhances the appreciation of natural scenery rather than detracts from it. Certain times of day are associated with certain sights and sensations. To be fully tuned into the outdoor world, one needs a heightened awareness of time, not a heedless forgetfulness of it. Alan Gussow has written perceptively of a "sense of place." We would add that a "sense of time" is equally crucial to a full awareness of the distant places.

"To every thing there is a season, and a time to every purpose under the heaven," it is written in Ecclesiastes.

For example, the time for high mountain vistas is incomparably the early morning or late afternoon, when the angle of the sun is so low as to throw into sharp relief the shadows of every ridge and fold, bringing out the noble and infinitely varied contours of the endless hills. If a good day is in the offing, white river mist may linger in each lowest valley, further accenting the lines of the main mountain ridges. Sometimes, if the day has been stormy and cloud-wracked, the late afternoon may bring an unexpected break, through which the healing sunlight pours. John Milton knew such moments in the English landscape:

> If chance the radiant sun, with farewell sweet,
> Extend his evening beam, the fields revive,
> The birds their notes renew, and bleating herds
> Attest their joy, that hill and valley rings.

Sunrises and sunsets themselves are special moments, their pageantry well celebrated by nature writers over the centuries. Frank Woolner has called dawn "not only a physical thing, it is an emotional birth." Sir Henry Newbolt referred to "the sacred wine of dawn." John Masefield, appreciating the seascapes he preferred, wrote of "a grey mist on the sea's face and a grey dawn breaking." In *The Bridge of San Luis Rey*, Thornton Wilder asked: "For what human ill does not dawn seem to be an alleviation?"

The loneliness of wild places at dawn, a result of the near-universal tendency of *Homo sapiens* to sleep late, adds to its appeal for the few who will get up with the thrushes. Tired of crowded hiking trails? You can have them all to yourself for about 20 percent of the peak summer vacation season from 5 A.M. to 8 A.M. daily, even on the Fourth of July. Aldo Leopold wrote:

> At daybreak I am the sole owner of all the acres I can walk
> on. It is not only boundaries that disappear, but also the
> thought of being bounded. Expanses unknown to deed or
> map are known to every dawn, and solitude, supposed no

longer to exist in my country, extends on every hand as far as dew can reach.

We'd back one step further each direction and sing the praises of those predawn and postsunset twilight hours. We love that gloomy elemental half-light period, especially in damps and mists, or with a high wind in high country, when the white-throated sparrow sounds his unforgettable, brave, clear notes amid the subalpine thickets. Of the postsunset murky hour, the poet Longfellow wrote:

> The day is done, and the darkness
> Falls from the wings of Night
> As a feather is wafted downward
> From an eagle in his flight.

But it doesn't. Anyone who has been out overdue on a walk as darkness comes on knows that night doesn't fall. It rises out of the ground from under thick woods. It wells up beneath the dark trees, the thick-branched evergreens first, and, after milling around for some time in the dense forest, gradually steals out into the clearings, keeping close to the ground. Only gradually does it rise and envelop people and the works of people. It hugs the shores of lakes and rivers, then slowly ventures out over the black waters. The sky is where it reaches last. Long after the earth is under its spell, the sky still holds out in brightness, save that a single gleaming jewel of a star foretells the end of light.

But enough of half-light. The middle of the day can have its moments of glory, most especially on those intensely bright midwinter days of splendor. No blue is ever so compelling as that of the zenith seen against a sharp-rising ridge of snow overhead. No air so crisp, but at about 10:30 in February.

So when we're in the woods and hills, we regard time as a vital element in the spirit of wildness. We don't forget time, we prize it. We try to treasure each time of day for its special qualities. We heed the words of Thomas Mann:

Hold fast the time! Guard it, watch over it, every hour, every minute! Unregarded it slips away, like a lizard, smooth, slippery, faithless, a pixy-wife. Hold every moment sacred. Give each clarity and meaning, each the weight of thine awareness, each its true and due fulfillment.

16

Solitude amid the Multitude

For solitude sometimes is best society.
JOHN MILTON, PARADISE LOST

MOUNTAIN SOLITUDE: is it lost and gone forever?

Many hikers deplore the loss of solitude, especially when they've just shouldered their way through the crowds on the summits of, say, New Hampshire's Mount Washington or Colorado's Pike Peak or even lordly Mount Rainier on a good day when all those guided parties stream up and down. Solitude seems as unattainable as the Holy Grail when you arrive late at a popular campground to find all available tent sites taken. We've joined in many a trailside conversation with old-timers who speak of long-gone days camping alone at once-secluded spots where they now find 40 people crowded in regularly on weekend nights. Even up in the Alaska Range, a spot on the once quiet and lonely Kahiltna Glacier is now nicknamed the "Kahiltna International" because of the steady parade of planes landing and taking off, and the little city of base camps erected by their clientele.

The feeling of solitude is vital to the enjoyment of the mountain experience. Most people go to the hills to get away from city crowds, to drink deep draughts of nature's cool wildness. Sitting alone on an alpine summit, with rolling forested ridges dropping away on all sides, no sign of man in any direction, is a unique and priceless aspect of wildness.

After a typical summer's trip in the popular mountains of New Hampshire or Colorado or the Northwest, many are inclined to pronounce obituaries for solitude.

We are sympathetic with this lament, yet we must disagree with the pessimistic premise on which it is based. We'd like to show in this chapter that mountain solitude is available in any mountain or backcountry area, any time of year—if you really want it.

The point is of more than academic or sentimental interest. Some of the authorities in charge of wilderness areas are using the lack-of-solitude misconception as a basis for considering regulations that would deprive hikers of that other precious ingredient of the wilderness experience: the freedom of the hills. If some of these plans go through, you won't be able to hike when and where you want because of complex and stifling rules and permit systems imposed in the name of solitude.

Some managers have even proposed making certain trails one way only, like city streets. The rationale is that if everybody's going up Trail A and down Trail B, they'll see each other less frequently.

Permit systems already exist in some areas. Maybe they are necessary in extreme cases. Many outdoorspeople approve of them. Where environmental impact requires limiting numbers, most people will go along with the idea. But where solitude is the goal, let's consider a moment.

Many hikers would be willing to give up some of their freedoms if they are persuaded that restrictions are necessary to preserve the experience of solitude. But our point here is that solitude is most assuredly available almost any place, any time, for those to whom it matters; therefore, restrictions on freedom are not justified on these grounds. Moreover, the sense of freedom is equally essential to a rewarding wilderness experience.

To be sure, if you like crowds in your "wilderness experience," you can find them. If you've been having any difficulty, we present herewith a list of 10 places in New England where you can "get away from it all" in a thoroughly sociable way—the backwoods equivalent of "tourist traps":

1. Mount Washington	6. Vermont's Long Trail
2. Mount Chocorua	7. Mount Mansfield
3. Allagash River	8. Mount Monadnock
4. Appalachian Trail	9. The Franconia Ridge
5. Mount Katahdin	10. Tuckerman Ravine

Others could supply similar lists for Colorado or California or wherever you plan to go.

There: are all of the crowd lovers headed for those 10 pleasure spots? Now, for the rest of you, here are four cases that illustrate why we say solitude is still available.

Case 1

On July 4, 1976, the most crowded holiday of the summer season and the Bicentennial year to boot, we went to the most popular mountain area in the Northeast, maybe the whole country: New Hampshire's Presidential Range. We were camped just below treeline. We got up on July 4 and strolled up the popular Randolph Path to the summit of Mount Jefferson, third highest in the Presidentials; this climb took an hour and a half, during which we saw not one other climber. We sat on the summit for a half hour, with nobody else anywhere in sight. Remember, this is July 4. Then we meandered slowly down the long ridge known as Jefferson's Knee, studying alpine flowers, many of which were in bloom. We descended the spectacular Six Husbands Trail, which some people rate as one of the finest hiking trails in the Northeast, into the Great Gulf Wilderness. There, after *four hours* of hiking, we came across the first other people we had seen that day.

Mountain solitude? You bet! Plenty of it, right there on the Presidentials on a splendid July 4. How come? Simple! We got up at 5:00 A.M. and were on the trail at 5:30. This may well be the most beautiful time of day in the mountains, but apparently very few people care to get up that early. Sunrises can be even prettier than sunsets—and lonelier. You can count on solitude during those magic hours on any mountain, any time of year. Later on that same July 4, we counted 117 other hikers on a three-mile stretch of trail. But from 5:30 to 9:30 A.M., we didn't see a soul.

For the first three hours of daylight, all hiking trails are dependably people-free, all summer long. If you figure on an average of, say, 15 daylight hours during summer months, that means a generous 20 percent of the entire summer is available for solitary rambling. And in many ways they're the nicest three hours of the day.

Oh well, you say, but nobody wants to go to the trouble of getting up that early. Our response is that it's a matter of values. If you really want solitude you don't mind getting up early. Nobody has to, but don't tell us that solitude isn't available just because most people like to sleep late.

Case 2

Three of us left the famous Lakes of the Clouds area on Mount Washington one day at the decadent hour of 9:30 A.M. At those lakes, at 5,000 feet, the Appalachian Mountain Club maintains a hut that's normally packed with guests, but on this day there were no guests and no hut crew within miles; just us three. We climbed Mount Washington and sat on the summit in bright sun, eating lunch, and seeing not one other person. We then traversed over Mount Clay to Mount Jefferson, without seeing a solitary soul. On our return to the lakes, we passed two other people, the only people we saw during that entire day.

Mountain solitude? You bet! Right there on Mount Washington, all day, in spectacularly fine weather. How come? Simple! The date was March 14. Quite properly, very few people venture above treeline in the dead of winter. The weather can be atrocious. The combination of intense cold, high winds, and low visibility can kill in a matter of minutes if you're not fully equipped with winter climbing gear, experience at dealing with such conditions, and sense enough to hole up when the weather turns bad. On the day before and the day after our beautiful day on Washington and Jefferson, above-treeline travel was unthinkable. We just burrowed into our down sleeping bags and sat it out until the good day came. All three of us had extensive experience in being browbeaten by White Mountain weather at its worst.

But, apart from the specialized world of winter climbing, we don't all have to climb Mount Washington in midsummer or on Labor Day weekend. The fall is a superb season for hiking. And the fact remains that anyone who really values mountain solitude can find it in abundance if he is willing to learn what it takes to travel in winter among the high peaks.

Case 3

On three successive days in mid-July we climbed three of the loveliest mountains we've come across in New England, passing but one other party low down on one of the three and not seeing anyone else otherwise. We hiked the standard trails on these mountains and didn't get off to any early-morning starts.

Mountain solitude? You bet! We had the summits and trails all to ourselves. How come? simple! These three mountains were off in obscure corners of Maine where the hiking crowd doesn't realize yet that there are some great places to go. We're not mentioning the names of these three peaks, because we don't want to set them up as targets for everyone who reads this book, but there are plenty of such places—marvelous hiking trails that no one much uses.

You can find your own secret places. Just get a map or two and start exploring. But tell it not in Gath, publish it not in the streets of Askalon.

Case 4

On a popular summer weekend, we descended from a camp high in the Presidentials, leaving our camp at about 9:30 A.M. and reaching the road sometime after noon. This was not early in the morning, but in broad daylight. It was not the dead of winter, but, as we said, a popular summer weekend.

Mountain solitude? You bet! Didn't pass a single hiker during the entire trip out. How come? Simple! We descended a little-known and little-used trail, not one of the standard trade routes that everybody seems to congregate on. This trail is right in the popular Presidential Range, is on every map of the region and in every guidebook, and there are plainly visible signs at junctions with other trails and at the road head. But it just happens to be one that very few people choose to travel. As a result, it's a narrow, twisting trail over lovely moss-covered boulders and logs through lush growth of ferns and dark, quiet stands of spruce. By contrast, most of the popular trails show distinct wear.

Nothing prevents anyone from using this trail (whose name we're not mentioning, you notice). It's just that most of the time, on the popular mountains, 90 percent of the foot traffic goes up and down two or three well-known trails. Most people apparently *want* to travel the familiar routes where they'll meet everyone else. The hills are full of out-of-the-way trails where you can find beauty, quiet, and solitude anytime.

This leads us to an observation that we wish backwoods managers would note carefully: Most "wilderness" recreationists apparently don't really want to be alone. Sure, they want to get away from the city, and they seek some reasonable degree of solitude, if solitude can be said to have degrees. But they don't *really* want to be completely alone out there, as evidenced by the small number of people who avail themselves of the ample opportunities for 100 percent solitude to be found in the early hours, or on little-used trails, in out-of-the-way mountain ranges, in bad weather (if you learn to like all-day rains, that's a great time to enjoy popular mountains by yourself), or in seasons of the year that others shun.

Of course, if you just abandon trails and take up the arcane art of bushwhacking with map and compass, you can get away from people even in the most popular ranges. You may tear your trousers in the puckerbrush, your pace may slow to a quite literal crawl, and you may even get thoroughly lost from time to time, but it all depends on what you're looking for in the mountains. On one splendid July 4, three of us climbed New Hampshire's Franconia Ridge. A steady stream of crowds walked the trails that day, but we chose to leave the trail, follow up a close-grown stream bed, clamber up long slabs of steep open rock, pass briefly over the crest of the ridge (momentarily amid the crowds there), then plunge down a long dirt-and-scree slide on the other side, and out through trailless woods. Except on the ridgelines trail and at the very beginning and end of the trip, also on trail, we passed no one—*on July 4.*

The fact is that many outdoorspeople speak wistfully of getting away from the people, far from the madding crowd, but they make no real effort to do so. In fact, just the opposite. Many Shawangunks rock climbers deplore the overcrowding of that climbers' paradise, yet persist in climbing at the densely populated Trapps or Near Trapps, ignoring the existence of miles and miles of marvelous cliffs where almost no one ever goes. Backpackers will head for the shores of Lake Colden or the confluence of trails in the Great Gulf, where they are assured of a flock of other tents, instead of veering just a bit out of the way to camp by themselves.

How many times do you see popular tenting areas overflowing with people, all camping within a couple of acres, when vast stretches of woods on either side go unoccupied? People must prefer the social experience of talking with other campers, comparing tents, and perhaps engaging in a bit of one-upmanship about their equipment or their experiences.

One summer at a roadside campground near Moosehead Lake in Maine, we found about a dozen campsites in a large open field, plus three secluded spots off in a little woods by themselves. When we arrived, we found all but one or two of the field sites occupied, cheek-by-jowl—but none of the three secluded spots (until we took one).

If this is true—that people like a little company with their "wilderness"—then the implications for backcountry management are interesting. Surely there is far less need to infringe on everyone's freedom in the name of preserving an experience of solitude.

For example, we'd take a dim view of declaring certain trails one-way-only so that hikers don't encounter as many other hikers, when it's perfectly possible to walk those trails for hours without seeing anyone else—from 5 to 8 A.M., for example—or to hike on other trails that the multitudes voluntarily seem to avoid.

We chafe at the idea of requiring permits to enter wild areas in order to preserve a "wilderness experience." In the first place, we question whether campers really want to be alone when they all flock to the same mountains, via the same trails, stopping at the same campsites. In the second place, anyone who does value the experience of solitude can get it, as we do, by the methods we've been indicating. But permit systems arbitrarily clamp down on where and when you can travel. When all the permits have been handed out, you can't go into the area.

What an irony: under a permit system, you could be prevented from getting mountain solitude in certain areas by the very rules designed to promote that solitude! As Phil Levin wrote in *Appalachia* magazine: "It would be ironic if we saved wilderness from the exploiters only to lose it to the managers and the masses. It could happen."

We don't mean to imply that overcrowding is not a problem in the Northeast woods. It certainly is, and it results in terrific problems of trail erosion and soil compaction at popular camping areas. Whether permit systems are justified to reduce the impact of sheer numbers is another question; we're simply saying that permits and other restrictions on freedom are not justified in the name of solitude.

Solitude is of the essence of wildness. If we lose the opportunity to be alone in remote places we may never get it back. We're for maintaining opportunities for solitude at almost any cost—but it's not yet time to destroy the freedom of the wilds on these grounds.

Case Study

Winter above Treeline

If I ever die, I want to die in Chicago.
MINNIE MINOSO

THIS IS A TALE that almost became a tragedy.

It's about the brutal cruelty of the mountain gods in winter-time—though on this occasion they chose to spare their helpless victims, perhaps to see if they could profit from the experience.

It's a story worth retelling for the lessons it teaches about winter camping and climbing in New England mountains.

The day after Christmas, 1968. A father and his 16-year-old son started on a trek through New Hampshire's White Mountains by struggling into huge packs and snowshoes and slowly plodding through a couple of feet of fresh snow up a mountain trail called the Valley Way. Whoever named this trail had his terminology on backward: The "Valley" Way climbs nearly 4,000 vertical feet in less than four miles, up into the northern end of the Presidential Range.

Their objective was to traverse the peaks of the Presidentials, and if possible to continue on across other mountain ranges to the west. They never got near those western ranges. The Presidentials

177

taught them several lessons, which we'll try to enumerate as the story goes along.

Father and son got about three miles that first day. Besides a late start, their packs were jammed full of enough winter equipment and food to last them 10 days, and this was before the day of much lightweight gear. The packs weighed over 80 pounds apiece. The fresh, unconsolidated December snow conditions, plus the weight of those packs, meant that at every step the lead man sank in about two feet. It was absurdly slow going.

Lesson 1: Don't count on moving rapidly in winter. Trail conditions can make half a mile per hour an exhausting speed. The Appalachian Mountain Club suggests, "Guidebook travel times should be doubled in winter." Under some conditions, that advice is not nearly conservative enough.

That night, they camped right on one of the few level spots in the trail and watched the temperature sink to –12°F. In the morning it was -18°. But so far they were doing OK, and soon they continued successfully till they emerged above treeline in the Presidential Range in the high col between mounts Adams and Madison.

Here the full fury of the notorious Presidentials' winter was tuning up. Winds shrieked and howled, buffeting the two climbers at every step. Temperatures below zero in a still valley feel darn cold; those same temperatures on an exposed, wind-racked ridge are of an entirely new order of cold.

A curious feature of the Presidentials in winter is that much of the alpine zone has relatively little snow on the ground. That is due to those ferocious winds, which blow most of it clean off the treeless heights, leaving a frozen terrain of rocks, ice, and very hard-packed snow. Where wind currents permit snow to collect, occasional vast snowfields build up to considerable depth, covering every feature of the mountain and every trace of the trail. Aside from these great snowfields, though, New England's most wintry winter spot paradoxically does not have very deep snow.

Father and son came prepared for this environment. They changed snowshoes for crampons. They pulled windproof nylon pants over their regular wool pants. They donned face masks, around which parka hoods were pulled tight, and "monster mitts" that extended up to their elbows. No flesh must be left to that punishing wind.

Lesson 2: Bring clothing suitable for full-scale arctic conditions. Especially important is adequate headgear (because so much heat loss occurs through the head), genuine winter boots (*not* summer-weight hiking boots), and a good mitten-glove combination.

Our two climbers managed to reach the two nearest summits, mounts Madison and Adams, by leaving their heavy packs lower down on the ridge and dashing up to the summit and back with just ice ax in hand. The air was crystal clear, and the sky an unbelievably deep blue, so they had no difficulty in finding their packs again each time they came back down from the summits, a fact they were to recall with grim irony 24 hours later.

That night they reached the col between mounts Adams and Jefferson, where they huddled into a small emergency shelter that was maintained there by the Forest Service.

In the morning the temperature had risen to 12°F. Visibility was socked in and light snow was falling, but the wind wasn't knocking them off their feet anymore, so they made the decision to proceed. Their trail was to slab the broad shoulder of Mount Jefferson, then continue toward Mount Washington, the largest peak in the Northeast.

The decision to move on in those conditions proved to be a dangerous mistake. Visibility was soon no more than 50 feet. Furthermore, it became obvious that they had underestimated how much wind they would be dealing with as they moved out of the col. They had scarcely started when it became evident that a full-blown winter storm was under way.

Climbing out of the col onto the side of Jefferson proved to be hard work under those conditions. Laboring under heavy packs, they became quite warm and shed their wool shirts from under their wind parkas. The father decided that uncovering his pack to stow the shirt inside would risk frostbite to his fingers, so he just tucked the shirt securely under the top flap and resumed the arduous climb.

As they rounded the shoulder of Jefferson, they began to traverse one of those huge snowfields that collect on the Presidentials in winter. This snowfield is visible from the highway well into July most years, so its depth in midwinter is obviously considerable. In fact, it covers almost every cairn or other trace on the trail.

With low visibility, it became difficult for the two climbers to stay on trail. Then, as they came out of the lee of the summit, the full fury of the wind slammed into them, blowing a steady torrent of ice crystals into their faces. Progress became painfully slow. To guard against losing their way—which could have been disastrous—the son would go out from the last identified cairn as far as he could and still see it. Then the father would go out from there as far as he could without losing sight of the son, and stand there waiting for some brief lapse in the wind to try to squint forward into the fury of the storm in a forlorn effort to find another cairn. In all that snow, however, only the tops of the tallest cairns showed, and often many minutes passed before they could spot the next one and move on.

To one who has not been up there, it is difficult to convey the full import of a winter storm above treeline. The myriad of unfamiliar sensations include:

- Barely being able to stand on your feet, braced always by your ice ax, and moving forward fitfully only between gusts
- The unrelenting din and tumult of the wind, so loud that you must shout virtually into your companion's ear to be heard
- The featureless enigmatic whiteness created by the unrelieved snow, ice crystals, and cloud, which surround you on all sides, up and down
- The sense of every little procedure being enormously difficult and time-consuming (even looking at your watch, for example, involves uncovering that wrist from the monster mitt, parka, and shirt, then painstakingly getting

them all snugly back together—it perhaps shouldn't take so long to do, but up there it does)

All of these sensations are exciting enough if you step out into them for a half hour. If you're out in them for several hours, they'll wear you down. If you're out in them all day long and no prospect of escaping them at night save in a tiny tent somehow staked up there, you have to learn to take it as a way of life.

Admiral Byrd, caught in an Antarctic blizzard, described it in *Alone* as "extravagantly insensate":

> Its vindictiveness cannot be measured on an anemometer sheet. It is more than just wind: It is a solid wall of snow moving at gale force, pounding like surf. The whole malevolent rush is concentrated upon you as upon a personal enemy. In the senseless explosion of sound you are reduced to a crawling thing on the margin of a disintegrating world; you can't see, you can't hear, you can hardly move.

It is this scene which the jealous winter gods of Mount Washington aspire to imitate. Sometimes they do a pretty good job.

Eventually the father and son did get across the snowfield and out onto the southern slopes of Mount Jefferson, where once again they could stumble on blown-clear rocks and ice, where cairns were at least visible from time to time, when the wind-driven ice would permit them to steal a look ahead.

Lesson 3: Never try to move in a full-scale storm above treeline. These two should have stayed put in their shelter for a day, as they were to do in an even greater storm later. No one should risk becoming exhausted or lost in a snowfield in the incredible and relentless fury of those White Mountain storms.

When they got to the far side of Jefferson, the cloud cover momentarily lifted, revealing a gentle slope angling up to the summit of Jefferson. The two climbers could not resist the lure of the summit. They had already bagged Madison and Adams; they had to grab Jefferson while they had the chance. Dropping their packs, they decided on a quick rush up to the nearly visible summit and back to their packs.

The climb went easily, and they delighted in the freedom of an easy dash uphill without packs and with the wind at their backs. When they landed on the summit and congratulated each other, the Mountain King stopped smiling and frowned.

The clouds came down again, the wind picked up. Father and son suddenly realized that they could not see more than a few feet; that they had lost all sense of which direction they had come up from, or which direction to descend; that the wind-driven snow had completely obliterated all trace of their tracks in a matter of minutes; that each rocky outcropping on the mountain looked like all the others; and—the crushing blow—that the father's compass, which he always carried handy in his wool shirt pocket, was right there: in the wool shirt that he had so carefully tucked in the pack, which now lay down there on the trail somewhere below them.

How can you be lost when you know just where you are (in this case, the very summit of Jefferson, at 5,715 feet, in a howling, screaming, swirling thicket of fog and driven ice crystals)? For several minutes the two tried to remain calm and move about the summit slowly, trying vainly to get some sense of which way anything lay. Calm and rational discussion is difficult when to make yourself heard you must stand right up against the other person's ear and bellow at the top of your lungs.

At length, they agreed on their best guess as to the way down and resolutely plodded ahead. After an eternity, repeatedly suppressing fears that they might be going in the wrong direction, they were overjoyed to see the sight of one of the cairns of the trail that they had been on before. But when they arrived there, they were soon able to figure out that they were back now on the north side of the mountain—which meant that in their careful calculations as to which way to descend from the summit, they had been precisely 180 degrees off course!

Now they had once again to face the risks and difficulties of crossing that same snowfield. Their tracks were, of course, long since wiped out in the wind-driven snow. Now, furthermore, the wind had considerably increased, the snow lay deeper (covering more of the cairns), and they were much, much more tired after all the buffeting they had already taken at the hands of the storm. They did manage somehow to swim or sink or wade or flounder across the snowfield. Finally, out of the implacably swirling cloud and snow, they once again saw ahead of them on the trail their packs, now all encrusted with snow and ice.

Lesson 4: Never go anywhere without a compass. It is hard to imagine getting turned around 180 degrees on a familiar summit, but it happened in this case and it can happen again. Once you lose that all-important sense of the direction of things, that alpine world up there suddenly appears featureless and inscrutable—and totally hostile. Without a compass, you're dead lost, body and soul.

Lesson 5: Don't count on following your own footprints. The wind can blow them to oblivion in a minute or two. The hole left by an ice ax lasts somewhat longer, so look for those rather than your crampon tracks—but nothing lasts long in a serious Presidentials' gale.

Lesson 6: Never separate yourself from the equipment you require for survival. These two reckless but lucky adventurers eventually found their packs again before being overcome by fatigue, darkness, or just plain inability to find their way in the storm. Without their packs—and spare clothes, sleeping bags, tent, stove, food—they would surely have perished in the open. With their packs, their chances of at least surviving anywhere were considerably improved.

All of these exhausting perambulations not only left both father and son fatigued but also consumed a considerable part of the available daylight hours. It soon became clear to them that they had neither strength nor daylight left in which to climb the enormous summit cone of Washington—over 1,000 feet of elevation—on which the fury of the wind would certainly increase.

Lesson 7: Remember that early winter days have the fewest daylight hours. As Yogi Berra said, it's the time of year when it gets late early. This fact should be kept in mind in all winter trip planning.

The prospect now confronted them of trying to set up a camp in which they could survive a night immobilized in this awesome storm. Having come this far, they were now many miles of formidable mountain terrain from any trail that led down out of the alpine zone to a nearby road. The only trail near them was the Sphinx Trail, which led sharply down into a vast wilderness area known as the Great Gulf, through which they would have to lug themselves and their enormous packs for many miles, in several feet of unbroken, unconsolidated snow, the depth of which must have considerably increased during this storm. That course could probably not be done in one day, and in any case would mean a total defeat to their plans, and perhaps two hard days of dispirited plodding through the woods to safety.

So they felt themselves strongly committed to sticking out the storm. Perhaps it would die down during that night and the morning. (Mountaineers tend to be ridiculously optimistic when all nature is screaming evil tidings at them.) They noticed at least that the temperature felt warmer, and mistakenly took that to be an encouraging factor.

Dropping a bit below the crest of the ridge, they carefully selected a spot in the lee of some large rock outcroppings, where they laboriously leveled a site for the tent. As they got the tent up, they noticed that the snow had changed texture—in fact, it was more like a sleet or freezing rain. The temperature had indeed climbed, but that meant trouble, not relief.

They managed to get set up inside the tent just before darkness. Then the wind shifted. That night proved even more frightening than the day out there on the snowfield. The wind repeatedly swelled into great buffeting blows, at which the helpless inmates of the tent would grab its A-frame poles, trying to hold it together against the force of the tempest, wondering how long the fabric would hold up against this punishment. Fortunately it did last through the night, but just barely.

In between the worst gusts of the storm, the father spent a full hour methodically scraping the encrusted ice and snow off his wool shirt, which had sat exposed on the outside of his pack during the day. He correctly reasoned that it would be vital to survival, since down garments lose their value as they get wet, and thus the time spent cleaning the ice off his shirt was a good investment. But the price of lost sleep was a stiff one to pay.

Lesson 8: Always take the time to pack essential items properly. In this case the price was only lost sleep. In other cases failure to stash an item inside your pack can result in its becoming so soaked as to be useless for the rest of the trip—or at the worst it can be torn off the pack unnoticed, and turn up missing when it's needed.

Early the next morning, the wind finally wore down the battered tent. Shortly after daylight, a brief but unmistakable ripping sound announced that the outer fly had given way. Within seconds, it was reduced to tattered shreds flopping noisily at the downwind end. Father and son knew that it was an unnecessary question to ask how long the main fabric of the tent might hold out.

Lesson 9: In setting up a tent, never assume that the current wind direction will necessarily hold constant. As a matter of fact, it is tempting to make the generalization that no tent made can stand up to the fury of a Presidentials' storm at its worst. You're better off not putting your confidence in any above-treeline shelter if you have no easy escape route. Snow caves or igloos offer a better chance for survival, but they are time-consuming to erect, can get you very wet in the process, and cost daylight hours that can probably be better spent getting to some less-exposed spot, preferably below treeline.

Somehow father and son got their tent dismantled and set off desperately to get down out of the wind. The Sphinx Trail proved extremely steep and difficult to negotiate with their gigantic packs. Between the time it took them to pack up, the difficulty of descent, and the formidably deep, soft snow they encountered down in the woods, they made very few miles that day, stopping for the night at one of the shelters that have since been removed from the Great Gulf Wilderness. By nightfall, the storm had abated. It stopped sleeting—but this only brought a new danger. All of their clothes had become wet, and now the temperature again began to drop.

Lesson 10: In winter, neither wind nor cold are as deadly an enemy as warmth and rain, followed by cold. When a winter storm turns warm and drops rain, that's the time to look out for your life. You'd better be prepared to get out of the mountains fast, especially if your clothes and other essential equipment have been getting wet. A sudden drop in temperature after a freezing rain can catch you with your defenses down.

As it was, this father and son spent their worst night yet shivering in down sleeping bags that had lost most of their insulating warmth from the soaking they had received. Both wore all of their clothes, but those big fluffy down jackets that had felt so warm a few days earlier now clung damp and clammy.

Lesson 11: Many layers of wool are worth the finest down gear when wetness is a potential problem. It's a mountaineers' cliché that wool is "warm even when wet." Most experienced climbers place little reliance on those big down parkas you see in the ads. Newer fabrics are now in widespread use that prove even more mountain-worthy. But this was 1968. And it remains true that a series of sweaters, shirts, and underwear, whether of wool or of the newer fabrics, are far more reliable than one monster parka when the chips are down.

Somehow they shivered through that night. The whole next day was spent in a dreary plod through bottomless soft snow, laboring under huge packs, oppressed additionally by the sense of having been totally defeated by the casual fury of what was only a typical period of bad weather in the Presidentials.

The foolish pair didn't know when to give up. After spending a morning in a laundromat, repeatedly dropping dimes (this was a quarter century ago!) in the driers till their sleeping bags and clothes were fluffy again, they set off at noon the very next day to climb directly up Mount Washington, this time using the eight-mile summer auto road for their route of ascent.

Along that road, where it rises above treeline, there were then, at half-mile intervals, a series of boxes for the emergency refuge of the summit weather observers on their trips up and down. Each one was roughly a cube, seven feet each way on the inside, with one double door for access and one double window for light. They were, needless to say, extremely well secured to the mountainside. These days the weather observers almost always ride up and down in a fancy snow machine, so the romance of risky foot travel is gone—and so are those emergency boxes.

Our intrepid pair reached one of those boxes at 5,500 feet on that afternoon of December 31. They did not leave again until January 3.

What happened was another storm, this one seemingly designed to make the earlier one look like a faint breeze. For three nights and two days it was unthinkable to move on that mountain. The summit weather observatory recorded winds of over 100 mph for 23 straight hours at one point, with peak gusts well over 150. The temperature dropped to -26°F on January 1 and ranged between -11° and -18° on January 2, warming up to a mild -3° on January 3.

Inside the box, father and son were far better off than in the previous storm, having learned to stay put. When they started their stove for a meal, the indoor temperature even got above 0°F (though never above 10°F). They lived inside their down sleeping bags.

Their biggest problem, besides boredom, was getting snow to melt for water. Any loose snow had long since been blown off into the next county. To get snow, one of the two would get dressed in full climbing regalia, including face mask, monster mitts, and crampons. Then the other would open the doors, and the first would hop out and wrestle the outer door closed while the second slammed the inner one shut. Ice ax in hand, the person outside would creep up the slope to where a cornice of hard-packed snow had accumulated nearby. There he would spread open a stuff sack, holding it open with one knee and one hand. Then he would strike the cornice repeatedly with his ice ax. At each blow, chunks of snow would dislodge and immediately be picked up and shot off by the wind—but some of them might land in the stuff sack. This process would be repeated until enough of the precious snow had accumulated in the bag to satisfy their water requirements for the day. Then the weary and frozen climber would creep back to the box, knock hard on the door and jump inside. The next half hour would be devoted to assiduously sweeping snow off sleeping bags and everything else, since opening the doors for even those split seconds resulted in filling the box with a thin coating of spindrift over everything. It was, of course, vital not to allow the snow to stay on the sleeping bags, where it might melt into and soak the down.

Boredom was combatted principally by resorting to the reading matter brought along in anticipation of the prospect of being pinned down like this. The son made out all right with some dime-store mystery stories. The father had made the mistake of bringing Dostoevsky's *Notes from the Underground* and a poetical translation of *The Iliad*. Such heavy stuff had absolutely no appeal in those surroundings and went unread.

Lesson 12: Sex and violence are the only reading matter able to command attention at 5,500 feet in a howling tempest. Can the culture.

They also ripped out the last 52 pages of a small memo pad and made an impromptu deck of cards. In the ensuing poker games, each used his precious lunch and snack items for chips. This resulted in a deadly serious game. When you are staking your last best candy bar on three nines, you've got to be sure they're winners! Even a small hard candy must have the support of a pair of face cards at the least.

On January 3, with the wind easing off to something in the general neighborhood of 50 mph, they managed to leave their box and struggle to the summit and back, later descending back down the road, much subdued and humbled by their vacation in the mountains.

Those two were lucky. They survived all their mistakes and inexperience. Others have been less fortunate.

Lesson 13: Never trifle with winter in the mountains. If you decide to undertake this special madness called winter climbing, prepare yourself well. Read up about it, get the correct equipment, but most important of all, hook up with someone who has experience in that unique world. Start slowly, with day trips only at first, then plenty of overnight experience below treeline, where you can learn to deal with the cold without the additional devastating problem of wind.

It's not just that the wind feels stronger and colder in winter. It *is* stronger. The average wind speed on Mount Washington in July is 24.7 mph; in January it's 43.8. From 1948 to 1975, the fastest wind recorded during July averaged 80.7 mph; during January it was 124.9.

Everybody knows where winds like these take you on those famous "wind chill" charts.

To repeat, the wisest procedure is to learn directly from more experienced climbing partners. Clubs like the Appalachian Mountain Club in the White Mountains, the Green Mountain Club in Vermont, and the Adirondack Mountain Club in New York State have organized programs for helping novices gain experience under counsel from those who have been through it all.

Above all, try to avoid the mistakes we've outlined above, which that foolish father and son encountered many years ago.

You can profit from mistakes, as they did. The son in our story went on to become an outstanding mountain climber, with "first ascents" in the Canadian Rockies and Alaska, including the East Ridge of Mount Huntington, the South Face of Mount Hunter, and the redoubtable 6,000-foot Southeast Spur of Hunter, all climbs of exceptional difficulty. The father went on to many more years of pleasurable winter climbing in the hills of New England, and wound up coauthoring this book with his wife, Laura Waterman.

17

Five Winter Trips: The End of Adventure?

The future of American wilderness depends on American civilization's deliberately keeping it wild.

RODERICK NASH,
WILDERNESS AND THE AMERICAN MIND

AS THE FOREGOING case study illustrates superabundantly, in the mountains winter *is* wildness, almost automatically. That is, the conditions facing the hiker in winter often guarantee adventure, dealing with nature on nature's terms. Yet even here a temptation arises to soften the wilderness experience, to compromise it, to dilute, to belittle, to emasculate.

A very real issue confronting the future of winter recreation is whether we are going to reduce the winter mountain experience to accommodate our limited powers and limited vision, or whether we are going to take it on the mountain's terms and rise to the challenge.

Five stories of winter mountaineering adventure illustrate the changing conditions of winter travel. Taken sequentially, they illustrate the progressive degradation of the mountain spirit when humanity imposes its own terms on nature.

Trip 1

In 1962 the first known attempt to traverse the White Mountains in winter was launched. Back then, climbing the Northeast's mountains in winter was tough. Very few people were coming to the winter mountains. Parties needed to break out on snowshoes nearly every trail they used. Some peaks with trails after 1970 were trailless before then. The Kancamagus Highway, which slices through the mountains from east to west, was not plowed, making many peaks in the interior far less accessible.

Then, safety was the watchword. Because of the remoteness and the inherent danger, these early winter climbers loaded themselves down with gear enough to confront any emergency, slouching cumbrously about in large parties. Consequently, they traveled very slowly. As one authoritative winter climber of the day stressed, "Safety must prevail over speed."

Inevitably, under all this weight and with the odds stacked so heavily against them, winter climbers set very limited objectives. Within those limits, that generation accomplished some impressive feats. Despite an underlying and perhaps inhibiting conservative approach, their boldness and love of adventure would not be suppressed.

In 1962 Robert Collin conceived the plan of traversing the White Mountains in winter. Collin was a winter trip leader who had learned and taught under the winter programs of both the Adirondack Mountain Club and the Appalachian Mountain Club. He had written state-of-the-art articles on winter backpacking. He was the acknowledged authority. The route he proposed would take his party past all of the Appalachian Mountain Club's high mountain huts, covering roughly 55 miles.

The demands of that trip in 1962 are difficult to envision today. Now two of those huts are kept open all winter, furnished with an efficient wood stove, and staffed by a caretaker. Then they were all closed and cold, no haven for the winter traveler.

In point of fact, there were times in the early days when the huts were left unlocked, but they remained unheated, and a big cold building is a doubtful asset in winter. You win protection from storm and insulation from snow, but you lose the cozy heat-retaining confines of a small tent. The coldest night we have ever spent in the "outdoors" was "indoors" at one of the AMC huts back in those days when they were left unlocked: Lincoln's Birthday in 1967, when the summit of Mount Washington reported -41°F , the top of Cannon -36°, and we were higher than Cannon, across the valley at Greenleaf Hut. We are not at all sure it was an advantage to sleep on the open floor of that cavernous, drafty hut, its wood floors creaking and snapping all night in the extreme cold. Probably we'd have been warmer in a tent, where our body heat would not have been dissipated fruitlessly. So whether Collin's party had access to the insides of the huts or not makes little difference, they were of such little value compared with the two that are open (and heated) today.

Furthermore, Crawford Notch, the halfway point of Collin's proposed trip, was without shelter of any kind. In those days a summer resort, the Crawford House, sprawled its elegant finery over the manicured lawns of the notch, but in winter all that luxury was boarded up tight. Wind sighed and whistled through the lifeless notch, in the same way it had when an 1850s traveler noted:

> For two-thirds of the year a more desolate place can hardly be imagined than this Notch. Dismal winds moan through the leafless trees, and through the fissures of the rocks.... Woe, then, to poor mortality, when the snow falls fast, and the king of tempests rides on the wings of the hurricane through the clouds, armed with winter's cold, blinding sleet, and avalanches of ice!

Between the huts, the trails (then much less carefully blazed) saw essentially no traffic. None. Zero. That meant Collin's party would have to break out every trail every day and not waste too much time by losing and refinding the trail. The physical demands of constant trail breaking and the steady pressures of trying to discern where the trail went was a trial few experience today.

More than the physical toll was the psychological burden of knowing they were the only folks out there. No help was at hand. Rescue techniques were primitive, but that wasn't important, because the main thing was that rescue was not likely to happen. The climbers were strictly on their own. This is a psychological burden that few experience today. The average winter climber of the 1990s may occasionally break out a new trail and can understand how tough it would have been to break trail every day. But those of us out there today, amid such a healthy population of other winter recreationists, cannot appreciate the psychological burden of being out there…all…by…yourself…

Collin proposed that his group traverse from west to east, ending their trip with crossing the Presidentials. They would be out for nine days, carrying all their food and gear, camping out each night. This meant toughing it out for the long slog up and over the Franconias and the humpy ridge to Garfield, across the Twin Range and Bonds in the remote Pemigewasset wilderness, through the Zealand Valley and out to Crawford Notch. And after that, a full winter Presidentials traverse, plus a jaunt up to Carter Notch.

If you just put your head down and doggedly kept placing one snowshoe in front of the other; if you could stand the hardship of your gear getting soggier and soggier, your down sleeping bag becoming less comfortable and certainly less effective as it picked up more and more moisture; if you could put up with little annoyances like constantly hitting snowy branches overhead with your overloaded pack, thus dumping snow on your head and shoulders and down between your back and your pack (in which warm spot it immediately turned to moisture and wetted further into your clothing); if you could stand the hardship of tenting out every night; then you could walk from Franconia Notch to Crawford Notch. As Collin said in one of his winter articles: "If you insist on being comfortable at all times you had better stay at home."

The Collin party did put their heads down and reach Crawford Notch, but here they met defeat. The Presidentials' famous winter winds can ruin the plans of even the most determined climbers. Collin and his group stormed the heights of the Crawford Path ridge. But there they were beaten back by relentless high winds and blowing snow. After an already-grueling struggle to reach Crawford Notch, they simply had no further resources to wait out a break in the weather. They had "lost."

Mountains 1, Hikers 0.

But what they had won was remarkable. Even though they failed in the ultimate objective, their "failure" was more notable than the success that occurred nearly 20 years later. Collin was out there when climbers took the mountains on their own rough and deliberate terms. He and his group were always breaking and finding the winter trail, often obscured in deep snow. Perhaps hardest of all, they carried the psychological burden of their isolation. A lot has changed in 30 years!

Trip 2

In the winter of 1968–69 came a second attempt. By this time the so-called backpacking boom had begun but had little affected the winter hiking population. As one measure, only about a dozen individuals had climbed all the 4,000-footers of either the White Mountains or Adirondacks in winter (compared with hundreds today), and no one had done both in the snowy season. Most trails remained untouched all winter long, the snow accumulating to great depth without the compaction of passing snowshoe trail or ski.

The year 1969 broke all records for depth of snow in New Hampshire. November 1968's snowfall as measured on the summit of Mount Washington was already 87 inches. December added another whopping 104 inches to the pile. Those records continue to stand, as does the record set in February 1969 of 173 inches. In all, that amazing winter, the total snowfall accumulation reached very nearly 50 feet! On the trails that led to and connected the AMC huts, an almost incredible depth of soft snow was building up even as early as November.

A party of four chose to deploy their resources in a new way so as to facilitate the winter traverse: one pair would start from Lonesome Lake and work eastward toward the Presidentials. The other pair would start at the Presidentials, do a standard Presidentials traverse, and then keep going. The two parties would meet roughly halfway. From then on the going would be easier because the trails would be packed. Or such was the elegantly worked-out theory.

On December 24, 1968, the first pair, Dave Ingalls and Roy Kligfield, started from Franconia Notch. With huge packs laden for the lengthy journey, they snowshoed up to treeline on the Franconia Ridge, crossed over the alpine zone and Mount Lafayette, and camped at Garfield Pond on that first night. Bitter cold temperatures and high winds greeted their efforts next morning, but they laboriously chugged on over Garfield and the ups and downs of that ridge, reaching Galehead Hut for a cold Christmas night. Ingalls had partially frozen a few toes the year before, and that night he noted ominous signs of recurring frostbite. Still determined, they took off from Galehead Hut and climbed South Twin. On the high wind-racked ridge beyond South Twin the snow had drifted so deep among the stunted trees that it was hopeless to find the trail. Repeatedly they sunk in "spruce traps" and had to struggle out of their enormous packs to extricate themselves. Ingalls realized his feet had lost all feeling. In desperation they opted to return to the lower and more sheltered elevation of Galehead Hut, where the temperature that night sunk to -24°F.

The next morning, December 27, the two climbers began a desperate flight for survival. They headed down and out, constantly losing and refinding the trail along the Gale River, physically worn and defeated, and with the certain knowledge that Ingalls's feet were in bad shape. By late afternoon they slid down the last snow bank to the plowed road. They didn't hitch a ride; they walked out in front of the next car and forced it to stop. Ingalls elected to be

driven to Massachusetts General Hospital in hopes of more knowl-
edgeable medical care there than at any north country hospital.
After a long recuperation, he walked back into the world with
several toes lost forever, a victim of frostbite.

The other pair included one of your authors, Guy, and his 16-
year-old son, Johnny. The preceding case study, "Winter above
Treeline" tells the story of their attempt—just as fruitless on their
end as the Ingalls-Kligfield fiasco.

Mountains 2, Hikers 0.

The second attempt to traverse the White Mountains in
winter was over. Obviously all four of us were totally and humiliat-
ingly defeated. Dave Ingalls had lost toes. The raw power, the
malign destructive force of a mountain winter had fully impressed
us.

Trip 3

In 1977 an ill-fated third attempt began. By this time the ground
rules had begun to change. Some of nature's advantage was neu-
tralized. That is, the Appalachian Mountain Club had opened two
of its high huts to wintertime use, installing a wood stove and a
full-time caretaker at both Zealand Falls and Carter Notch. The
volume of winter climbing had greatly increased, a fact that
implied that many trails were now regularly broken out. Still, the
real boom in winter climbing lay ahead in the 1980s, and many
other trails remained little used.

Again it was one of your authors, this time opting for the
adventure of a solo attempt. Going as spartan as I dared, I still had
a monstrously heavy pack, but the snows, while deep that year,
reached not the absurd depths of 1968–69.

The first day, February 3, after a quick packless ascent to
Lonesome Lake and back, I climbed Mount Lafayette finding a
welcomed packed-out trail to treeline. After I crossed the alpine
zone of Lafayette in moderately high winds, I plunged down into
the Garfield Ridge and found that no one had been there before

me. That trail was not as well maintained then as now. Repeatedly I lost and refound the trail. Within a short time I was exhausted and set up camp as a light snowfall began.

By morning fresh snow lay deep on the old surface and trees were drenched in new powder. On and off the trail I battled my heavy pack through the snow-laden forest, getting soaking wet in the process. Because of the energy required, I could keep warm in just a wool net undershirt and a 60-40 parka (the uniform of the 1970s winter climber), thus able to reserve my wool shirt and sweater for warmth in camp. Still, I was only able to go about five miles: in those days of unpacked trails many of us found that about five miles was a fairly standard maximum distance for a full day's vigorous effort. I camped again along the trail a half mile short of Galehead Hut.

That night I noted my sleeping bag getting damp and beginning to lose heating value. The parka and windpants, along with the net undershirt, were of course soaked through from the perpetual contact with snowy trees. I had a change of undershirt and dry wool shirt and sweater to wear in the tent. But if I were to have dry things for the next night, I had to be prepared to put the wet things back on in the morning. How to keep them from freezing solid? The parka and windpants I spread between the two foam pads I was sleeping on, so my body heat would keep them flexible. The net undershirt came into the sleeping bag with me: there it would dry out overnight, but of course its moisture would be transferred to the sleeping bag, further reducing its effectiveness.

On the next day I struggled up to Galehead Hut and South Twin. Along the ridge beyond I repeatedly lost trail and refound it. Even when I was on the trail I had to push through snow-laden branches all day long.

I noticed an interesting phenomenon. When I lost the trail, I would zigzag across the ridge, casting about to find it. Amid the dense scrub of the Twin Range, carrying a week's backpack, this was an utterly exhausting procedure. The compaction of the snow amid the conifers was completely unpredictable, randomly ranging from firm to plunging into your waist, with the not-infrequent surprise of plunging nearly to ground level, with six or eight feet of soft snow and interlaced evergreen branches as one's sudden neighbors. As I battled with this frustrating environment, I would push, push, push to keep fighting through the trees looking for the trail. Sometimes I'd spend as much as a full hour off-trail, making little progress. When I'd finally and unmistakably come across the trail, my mind would say: OK, you've lost time; now that you've got open sailing, make it up; full speed ahead! But my body, after unrelenting push, push, push through the spruce traps, would rebel. All of a sudden, though mentally thinking full speed ahead, I'd find myself achingly weary and lethargic, ready to rest.

Another five miles that day—with more physical strain than twenty-five in summer—brought me, at almost dusk, to the first sign of other human activity that winter since I had left Mount Lafayette more than 50 hours earlier: fresh snowshoe tracks just east of the top of Mount Zealand. I collapsed on them and immediately set up camp. My clothes were soaked from the contact with snow all day. The sleeping bag was now also distinctly clammy.

On the fourth day out, I followed the packed-out trail with unalloyed gratitude until I reached Zealand Falls Hut by late morning. Outside the hut, as I arrived in my encrusted parka and windpants, I met a nattily attired cross-country skier just placing his dainty boots in his bindings, the first fellow human I'd seen in about 72 hours. When I couldn't resist mentioning that fact, it brought no response. I had the impression that the idea of crossing the mountains alone for three days was so remote from the possibilities of his world (let alone the desirabilities) that he simply didn't take it in. I've since learned not to bring up my itineraries for those to whom they would only seem bizarre and certainly not sensible.

With my clothing and sleeping bag desperately wet, I surrendered to the availability of this island of fellow humanity's conveniences and spent three hours at the hut attempting to dry out enough for surviving one more night out. Then I continued on my way and reached the Ethan Pond area for my fourth night out. The pond proved a windy place, the temperature below 0°F, and my bag by no means completely dry. It was a shivery night.

The next day I stumbled down to Crawford Notch. There I fled for my car and home (and Laura). To have superimposed a Presidentials traverse on the exhausting trip I'd just completed was not to be thought of.

Mountains 3, Hikers 0.

It was a shrunken victory to have crossed from Franconia to Crawford Notch by myself in winter. The victory was cheapened by the use of the hut to dry out partially. And of course the big prize of also crossing the Presidentials Huts had been far beyond my reach.

Trip 4

In 1980 a party of three, the two of us plus a good friend of ours, Mike, set off to accomplish that traverse of the White Mountains. Remember: it was still the Last Great Problem, not yet accomplished.

But now a lot of the rules of the game had changed. Two of the Appalachian Mountain Club's high mountain huts were open in winter, provided with a warm stove, and staffed by a caretaker. Also, in that formerly wild and lonely waste of Crawford Notch, a cheerful AMC roadside hostel now glowed warm all winter, welcoming all winter visitors. Even more significant, the winter climbing boom was well underway. Snowshoers and skiers were starting to fan out all over the more popular trails. The taming of the mountains in winter was well advanced.

Of course your humble heroes were hard-line purists, and so was our friend, Mike. No indoor sleeping for us! No cheery stove or caretaker's care for us! We would carry our tent, a heavy three-person model, and camp in it *every night*. This would be our way of protesting the belittling of winter adventure that we saw represented by the opening of comfortable backcountry facilities in winter.

As in 1969, weather played a vital role in the outcome. The winter of 1979–80 was snowless, something unprecedented in our lifetimes. It meant very fast travel, sometimes faster than summer. Most trails were a sheet of ice, like a frozen sidewalk. That meant strapping on crampons for the whole day and striding along almost like summer. Deep snow was not obscuring the trailway, so trail finding was no problem whatsoever.

For our trio it meant fast going, which meant fewer days out, which meant lighter loads. With no snow, we didn't have to carry snowshoes, didn't have to laboriously break trail, didn't even have to find the trail. No snow would be knocked off branches by high packs to soak into clothing. Success seemed assured.

On day one we ran up to the hut at Lonesome Lake without packs, tagged it, and jogged down to the road again, then picked up our loads and started out. One hut down, seven to go.

It was a warm, overcast day with a forecast of rain, that dreaded scourge of winter mountain travelers. Before we'd reached Greenleaf Hut (number two) it began to drizzle. As we put on rain gear, we heard the wind picking up out of the south—a bad sign. We knew it would be a bit of a tussle to get over Mount Lafayette with its above-treeline exposure. It was.

The lightest member of our party was carrying a frame pack (well laden), and that pack acted like a sail, picking her up and setting her down rather roughly and not on her feet. Her biggest companion, Mike, would hoist her up by the top bar of the frame— equivalent to the scruff of the neck—stick a piece of chocolate in her mouth (for energy and morale), and we'd struggle on. After an hour's walking in something akin to the combined rinse and spin cycles of a washing machine, we reached the windblown and rain-pelted summit of Lafayette, continued on across to North Lafayette, and down into the shelter of the trees. Blessed trees! We still got wetter, but now we were out of that wind.

Wet: we know no rain gear made that can stand up to the punishment of wind-driven rain. We were soaked. At first we hoped to camp on Garfield Pond, but there we found half a foot of standing water. We resolved to press on through the dusk to shelter on the other side of Garfield. So much for purity! Well, we said, we'll camp out on all the other nights, we'll just use the shelter this first night to try to get dry.

The next morning we made an assessment. We were thoroughly soaked and highly vulnerable to any drop in temperature. In the old days, we simply could not have continued in our dampened state. We would unquestionably have aborted the trip. But in 1980 we knew that Zealand Falls Hut was open. Well, we decided, after we get really dry at Zealand then we'll be set and we'll use the tent every night and not go near those heated buildings. So on day two we slogged all the way to Zealand, tagging Galehead Hut (number three) on the way and making the last stream crossing in the dark. By the stove at Zealand, we felt warmth oozing in—and the adventure oozing away.

Well, funny thing: next morning we still felt damp in vital spots, especially sleeping bags. Also, our feet were sore from walking in inflexible crampons for two dawn-to-after-dark days. So we decided to make our third day a short one—sort of a rest day—and just go as far as Crawford Notch. Here we would finish the drying process at the hostel and rest up. This final drying should put us in excellent shape for tackling the Presidentials.

On day four, by now thoroughly dry at last, we marched up the Crawford Path to Mizpah Hut (number five). On we crunched over the Southern Presidentials. Things were getting exciting again. We were in the land above the trees, where anything can happen. We reached Lakes of the Clouds Hut (number six) about 2:30. Time for discussion: we could go on and camp someplace just the other side of Washington, like Sphinx Col. Or...we *could* stay in the basement room at the hut that is kept open by the Appalachian Mountain Club for winter backpackers. This basement refuge is not the Ritz: known to climbers as "the Dungeon," it is damp and dark, about three-quarters of the space taken up by two plywood sheets, one over the other, forming sleeping platforms. But the Dungeon has one distinct advantage: it is proof against the notorious Presidentials wind. When your ethics have been thoroughly eroded it gets easier to give into temptation.

The next day we were walking by seven o'clock. It was cloudy and blowy, but not too cold, a manageable day for the job, which was to cross the Presidentials. We were over four lofty summits and down to Madison Springs Hut (the second-to-last hut: number seven) by a few minutes after noon. The plan was to camp some place in the Great Gulf below—finally to use that heavy tent. But as we hurried down Madison Gulf Trail, we felt it was still too early to camp. As we kept walking, it came into our heads that we had a chance of getting to Carter Notch Hut (number 8 and last!) that night. What a day *that* would be—to walk from Lakes of the Clouds Hut to Carter Notch Hut via Madison in one winter day! We also had in mind that the welcome there would be warm: the winter caretaker, Peter Crane, had promised to bake a celebratory cake! We knew it would be past dark when we got to Carter, but, then, the sight of that hut and Peter's smiling face would be all the sweeter.

So that heavy tent never came out of the stuff sack.

Mountains 3. Hikers 1.

But a victory? Not really. Maybe we should stop keeping score. We don't think of a successful climb as defeating a mountain—on the contrary, it celebrates that mountain.

More important, it was perfectly obvious that our "success" was based completely on the shelter of five buildings, three of them heated. Had we not had warm stoves at Zealand and Crawford, we would have beaten a retreat after getting so wet the first day. We had definitely not taken nature on her own terms. We had simply passed quickly through the natural world to go from building to building.

Trip 5

In 1989 the final chapter in the sequence of five winter mountain trips was recorded. By now the rules of the game had changed still more. Now winter climbing was a popular sport; both snowshoes and skis crossed and recrossed all major trails all winter long. The two AMC huts were open, Crawford was a well-lit and -heated oasis, and the surrounding areas well populated. By now, too, the Randolph Mountain Club paid a caretaker to live in and supervise guests at Greyknob, a cozy cabin high on the flanks of Adams in the Northern Presidentials.

Now we decided to demonstrate graphically just how the terms of the mountain traverse had changed. Early in the winter one of us visited both the RMC's Greyknob and AMC's Zealand Falls Hut, talked with the caretakers, and secured permission to leave a small cache of food, mouseproof in a metal container, at each place. Cheating? Sure. But that was the point: to demonstrate how the open facilities, well-packed trails, and crowds of people had completely changed the wilderness experience from Collin's day and even our own previous efforts of 1968 and 1977.

On the morning of February 9 one of us snowshoed up the 1.6-mile packed trail to Lonesome Lake and touched the AMC hut. I carried only a small day pack containing a sleeping bag, a small supply of extra clothes, two lunches, and a few supper items, which would not need cooking. I went very light on first-aid supplies, but had parachute cord, tape, and a knife in case of needing to patch snowshoes. Total pack weight: 27 pounds. When I came back down to the road and started up Lafayette I encountered five or six other parties climbing Lafayette. It was below 0°F and blowing hard, so only one other party went to the top, as far as I knew. From there I turned north into the gale and began the traverse toward Garfield and the Twin Range. By the time I reached treeline on the Garfield Ridge I was glad enough to escape the punishment of the wind. Trying to be sure not to get dehydrated, I kept sipping water from my one canteen, secure in the knowledge that a vigorous stream flowed near the Garfield Ridge tent site shelter, a water supply I had often used in winter and never found frozen solid.

On the top of Mount Garfield I drained the last of my water and dropped down to the shelter in the last daylight. Consternation! And worse! That reliable stream *was* dry this particular winter. It had been a dry fall and late snow cover; the meager groundwater had simply frozen shut before the insulating snow cover came. When I dug down through the now-ample snow all the way to the ground, I found but dry stones. It was getting dark, still windy, I had no tent, and thus was reasonably committed to staying the night in the shelter.

So I stuffed my canteen completely full of snow and took it in the sleeping bag with me. I ate a completely dry supper that night, well aware of the dangers of dehydration in winter, with almost 50 miles yet to traverse. In the morning my canteen had melted barely enough water to dampen a bit of cereal. Then I packed up and snowshoed two waterless miles to a side trail that I knew reached a substantial stream, the Gale River, in just under a mile. I'd lose a lot of elevation and would have to come back up, but I simply had to have water. At the river I drank and drank, my body soaking it in with little apparent effect. Then I filled a full quart and climbed back up to my trail and continued on my way. That night, after 11½ miles and a lot of climbing, I reached Zealand Falls Hut.

Here was warmth, a crowd of people, the friendly caretakers—and my cache of food. I spent two nights here, soaking in the heat, water, and hot food, and spending the day between on a light-hearted bushwhack romp with the caretakers and Kita, their energetic canine friend.

On the next morning, again carrying two lunches and one cold dinner, I started early, crossed the Willey Range and was down for a morning cup of cocoa with yet another friendly caretaker at Crawford Notch. Then I climbed to treeline on the Presidentials.

Now came the only real question: Would the infamous Presidentials weather suffer me to cross unharmed? The temperature was moderately cold and winds reasonably stiff, but both manageable. As I passed above 4,400 feet or so, however, I encountered dense cloud, light blowing snow, and very low visibility. Crossing the heights of Mount Monroe, I was barely able to keep cairns in view. In the whiteout each projecting rime-covered rock could be mistaken for a cairn. I inched across, with that sense of being right on the edge of losing contact with where I was. Finally I recognized the summit rocks of Monroe and began the slow, difficult process of locating each cairn on the descent route, also coping with its steepness and an alarming tendency of the snow to form windslab over the old hard-frozen surface—a recipe for miniavalanches, which I must be absolutely sure not to start. (To have slid on that steep slope would have afforded enough speed to make the eventful collision with boulders somewhere in the whiteout below a most undesirable event, especially with no companions.) Eventually the surface leveled out and finally, a few feet away, the side of AMC's Lakes of the Clouds Hut loomed in the cloud.

After a night in the Dungeon, I set out in high winds and continued low visibility toward Mount Washington. It was desperately slow going for a while, but suddenly the clouds cleaved completely, and visibility went from 50 feet to 50 miles in a few seconds. Looking back, I could clearly see the Franconia Ridge on the horizon, whence I had come during the previous four days. Within minutes all the cloud was gone from Washington as well, and the summit buildings emerged clear against the deep blue sky. I half ran, half stumbled upward with delight, my feet warming with the exercise.

On the top of Mount Washington—on top of the world, I felt, at least my world of winter adventure in the Northeast—yet another form of cheating was available. Normally the Mount Washington Observatory makes it an absolute rule that there is no refuge for winter hikers on top. If they did not, they would be plagued with a multitude of visitors, many of them poorly equipped and more or less counting on help at the top. But by coincidence, Peter Crane, our host at Carter Notch in 1980, now happened to be working at the observatory that winter and had invited us to stop in for tea sometime. This I now did—in fact, I drank several cups of cocoa and filled my empty canteen with water. (We emphasize that this is *not* a generally available option; it is proper that winter hikers should be on their own resources completely on Mount Washington. Remember: part of the point of this trip was to be cheating.)

In high winds and cold, but with splendid visibility, I continued on across the Presidentials, climbing both Jefferson and Adams before dropping down the north flank of Adams to Greyknob and my next cache. Here was another sociable night with yet another friendly caretaker.

During the night the winds continued and the temperature dropped. I wondered, as morning approached, would the weather gods permit me to climb once more into their realm, so as to cross over the range, touch the seventh hut at Madison Col, and descend the other side toward the eighth and final hut at Carter? In the event, though the temperature was -14°F, and winds were measured up to 85 mph at the Mount Washington Observatory that morning, I had the wind largely at my back and, after the first half mile, also could put mountain mass between me and that dreadful wind. So I did make it across. Once down in the trees it was a shoe-in to the valley, my last cache of food (hidden in the woods at roadside), and up the easy 3.8-mile trail to Carter Hut.

Success? Well, yes. I crossed the mountains in winter with a 27-pound pack. But what did I personally achieve? Nothing terribly impressive. The feat was easily accomplished because I had so much help: open buildings for overnight shelter all the way, heat in some of them, friendly caretakers to visit, packed trails every foot of the way, plenty of other people around (at times). Most important was the psychological security of people, facilities, technology, escorting me all the way. It was not a wilderness experience. There were exciting moments; there were difficulties; there were times when I definitely had to think hard and work hard to ensure my own safety and success. But in no way was I strictly forced to rely on my own resources alone. I had help and support all around.

In every sense of the word Bob Collin's "failure" of 1962 was more impressive than my "success" of 1989, just as our three-person party's "success" of 1980 had been less of an adventure, less of an acccomplishment than that desperate struggle four of us had in 1968 or one in 1977.

Wildness is such a small thing in the Northeast. A very little tampering with it causes frightful ripples. It does not work to say,

You don't *have* to stay in the heated huts. Of course, we don't. But the mere fact that they are there changes the experience forever. One cannot ignore their presence. If they are there, one can never do what Collin attempted. One can never enter the woods and say, Now I am truly on my own. That bail-out retreat is always in the back of one's mind.

It is a subtle thing: the maintenance of the illusion of wildness. Here in the Northeast the line is very finely drawn. The game—and it is nothing but a game—is delicately played. If we want our wildness we must work for it. Decide where we want the line and hold it there.

But the erosion is so creeping. It is like the tide coming in, first a foot from your toes, then up to your knees, and in a short while over your head. You never saw it move, but you are drowning and there is no more wildness.

The environmentalist Jack Turner has warned:

We lost the wild bit by bit for 10,000 years and forgave each loss and then forgot. Now we face the final loss.

18

In Defense of Difficulty

No cross, no crown.

JOSEPH WOOD KRUTCH, HARPER'S MAGAZINE

A FEW YEARS AGO an Italian party used helicopters to help them climb Mount Everest. The mountaineering world was aghast. What was the object? Why not just build a gondola to the top? Of course, the flying machines couldn't land climbers on the summit of the world's highest mountain, but the helicopters did eliminate some of the risk and challenge. And risk and challenge is why climbers go to the mountains.

Challenge, at least—and for some, risk—is at the heart of American backpacking and hiking, from New England to the Sierra.

Why is the backpacker spending the night out there in the woods instead of at a modern motel? Why do we labor under 40 to 50 pounds over mile after mile of rough trail or bushwhack? Set up a flimsy tent or hammock in the pouring rain? Slap at mosquitoes and no-see-ums all day and night? Sleep in a soggy sleeping bag instead of between clean sheets? Try to cook a meal on uneven, muddy terrain, over either a tiny portable one-burner stove or a wood fire that alternates between being a smoke-belching inferno and almost out?

A verdict of insanity is tempting, but since many backwoodspeople show few other symptoms of mental distress during their regular workaday lives, one must conclude that they rationally choose to inflict these miseries on themselves. Why?

One could answer, Because the rewards of being in the woods outweigh all its inconveniences. We're more inclined to say, however, that the hardships are part of the reason why people go to the backcountry. The backwoods camper is seeking out difficulty. He is voluntarily thrusting himself into situations of challenge. He is, in his pedestrian way, seeking what Antoine de Saint-Exupéry, the great French aviator and author, conceived of as "that new vision of the world won through hardship."

Thomas Hobbes described "the privilege of absurdity" as that "to which no living creature is subject but man only." Backpackers sometimes seem to go further than necessary to prove Mr. Hobbes's point.

So why are some backcountry managers trying to make the backpacker's life too easy? We say, keep life difficult in the backcountry—that's why people go there.

Let's consider a couple of examples:

Crossing swollen mountain streams can provide some of the most hair-raising interludes along the trail. We recall with relish many a precarious crossing—teetering on narrow tree trunks over raging torrents of swift water, or hopping from boulder to moss-slippery boulder, occasionally dropping a boot (or more) into the icy waters. Great memories of exciting moments. Sometimes terrifying. Sometimes hilarious. Always memorable.

But there are sober, serious bridge builders at work in the backcountry who'd like to exorcise such moments from the backpacker's experience. These overeager engineers will slap a huge log bridge, complete with cement foundations on both sides, over any flowing water too wide to jump. Instead of experiencing an interesting challenge, the hiker just puts his head down and plods over a tailored bridgeway. The mentality that regards such offenses as trail "improvements" can only be achieved by cross-breeding a beaver with a deskbound colonel from the Army Corps of Engineers.

We should take lessons from our western hiking brethren. Out West, difficult river crossings are accepted as part of the game. In Alaska they can be really wild. Sometimes you even have to improvise a raft.

Yet land managers all over the country seem bent on eliminating the difficult stream crossing from our backcountry experience. Bridges over the Dry River near Mount Washington, on the Cascade Brook Trail in New Hampshire's Franconia Notch, or over a minuscule stream draining Katahdin near the Abol Campground in Baxter State Park are all illustrations of the bridge-builder mentality run riot, to the detriment of the hiker's experience.

This kind of thinking would have offered Michelangelo a can of spray paint to do the Sistine Chapel. Surely it would have made the job easier and safer. Wasn't that the point—just to get the ceiling painted?

Another challenge of the backcountry is the steep little rock "step" on a mountainside. When you have to scramble a bit, crawl up with hands as well as feet, maybe stop a moment to figure out how to negotiate a near-vertical 15 feet—that's the sort of challenge that makes a steep trail memorable.

Ah, but let us help you, sir (or madam), says the overeager trail crew. Out come the chainsaws, axes, even jackhammers. On the steep South Ridge of Mount Willey, in New Hampshire's Crawford Notch, where once we enjoyed scrambling up challenging little rock moves, we now confront massive wooden ladders with hand railings. Worse still, a few miles away on the Fishin' Jimmy Trail (one of the most moderate of the many trails in Franconia Notch), some oversolicitous trail "improvers" actually blasted steps in the rock to make it easier, in places setting square wooden steps into the rock itself. What a desecration! If we want to climb stairs, we'll go to the Empire State Building. Who goes to Franconia Notch to climb stairs?

The AMC's Backcountry Management Task Force put it well:

Risk is implicit in all backcountry recreation. It is naturally
present and is a desirable feature of the backcountry. While
the manager should work to educate users about the risks
involved in backcountry use, it is not his responsibility to
eliminate those risks.

Again, on the steep Wildcat Ridge Trail in the Carter Range,
across from Mount Washington, overzealous trail crews have taken
a big L-shaped slice out of a boulder that we recollect had made for
exciting scrambling. We asked the managers responsible for this
degradation how many people had died there. "None," was the
response. "Was there ever an accident here?" we asked. They
looked down in silence. We observed that our impression was that
where a bit of steep scrambling was involved, people tended to be
very careful. Not only that, but those little challenging rock steps
are the very things they remember most vividly about their trip in
the mountains. They're what lend zest and adventure to their
experience. You're doing them no favor by making it easy. Some
managers misread the hiker's temper, we believe. They think we
want it all Easter and no Ash Wednesday.

In truth, we hikers are not guiltless in this regard. We recently went on an adventurous bushwhacking trip into a remote
valley, where there are no trails or any evidence of man, rarely
visited by anyone. It's in New England (we'd rather not say just
where, to protect its pristine character), but we might as well have
been in the remotest forest of Siberia—or so we thought. As we
plunged through the untouched woods, feeling that sense of awe
and inspiration that only true wilderness brings, we came upon bits
of shiny red tape tied to trees at 100-foot intervals! What a sudden
end to our idyllic sense of wilderness! Vandalism in our loveliest
stretches of natural wild country!

These bits of shiny red tape were probably strung up in that
remote watershed by hikers planning a winter trip. It's often
considerably harder to find your way in winter, so climbers who
plan an ambitious outing in January will often scout it out in

September. A temptation is to mark the route by hanging tape on trees every 100 feet or so.

That's fine for the convenience of the hikers involved in that trip. But we wonder whether those individuals ever considered how their action might destroy the spirit of wildness for the next party.

In our view this marking of trails is a lamentable procedure for several reasons: it eliminates the challenge of staying on trail, which is one of the great adventures of winter climbing; it constitutes an inescapable reminder that others have been or will be there, thus destroying the illusion of solitude; and it is, to put it bluntly, a form of litter.

Incidentally, in the places we have seen these tapes, the safety argument is absolutely irrelevant. Those are trails or routes where anyone who got lost could simply follow his own snowshoe tracks back; none of them are sufficiently exposed to blow over so fast that you couldn't follow them back. It's not at all like wandering above treeline, where safety is a factor.

We believe in a maximum of freedom in the mountains, but only up to the point that one person's actions do not adversely affect another person's experience. Those who rag trails are destroying the most important attribute of adventure and the feeling of remoteness that others seek. Furthermore, in our opinion they're doing themselves no real service by eliminating the challenge.

Hank Aaron could have hit more homers had he stayed in the Little League all his life; his achievement is great only because he did it against the finest pitchers of his generation. The response to challenge is what made it all worthwhile. So too in the backcountry.

The late Hubert Humphrey once made a comment about life that applies with special force to this subject: "If anything's easy, it's not likely to be worthwhile."

Warren Doyle, an athletic young enthusiast who has set a speed record for hiking the 262-mile Long Trail in Vermont (nine days), may scarcely be a typical backpacker, but it may be instructive to note his comment on why he undertook his feat. Doyle was quoted as alienated by society's "striving for comfort, safety, plushness and such." He told a *Rutland Herald* reporter, Steve Baumann: "I've known failure and success in my hikes. When I succeeded, I knew it wasn't by luck. When I failed, I couldn't blame someone else."

Here is a proposition on which all lovers of the outdoor world ought to be able to agree. Hikers, hunters, birdwatchers, technical rock climbers, anglers, skiers, canoeists—all these and many more turn to the outdoors to find challenge, not ease; uncertainty, not security; "preferring hard liberty before the easy yoke of servile pomp."

Since different uses of the backcountry sometimes seem to conflict, we like to point out areas like this where we're all agreed.

Hunters? No hunter worth the name seeks an easy prey, with guaranteed success on the first day. The wildlife writer Frank Woolner has stated: "We would quit if the game were easy.... We respect our quarry, and we know that we will be humiliated in the field."

Respect, humility—that's what we're trying to talk about. We've climbed a lot of mountains, but we still have enormous respect for what these little New England hills can throw at you; yes, and plenty of humility about our own ability to get in trouble if we're not careful how we climb. If you can do it blindfolded, why bother? When they start providing graded paths and railings, we'll go somewhere else.

Birdwatchers? One of the most difficult things to do outdoors is to identify what species of warbler is flitting around in a grove of evergreens 50 yards away. There is no shortcut to finding out either; you have to invest hundreds of hours in the field, patiently stalking, listening, peering through binoculars at those perpetual-motion creatures no bigger than a small mouse but far more elusive. Like hunters, anglers, and mountain climbers, the avid birder is up before dawn to get out to where he needs to be when the winged mysteries start playing their games of hide-and-seek. But, oh, the rewards! If you've ever been standing next to someone who finally spotted their first blackburnian warbler on their own, you'll know a happy person.

Nor do the birdwatchers want it made easy. It's no accident that when you're recording birds on your "life list," you can't count caged-up birds from a zoo or private aviary. You've got to earn each one the hard way.

Anglers? From what we hear, the followers of Izaak Walton are happiest when the pickings are leanest. Bringing in some wily trout or bass that's eluded you all summer in some dark private pool seems to be the angler's prized moment. If the fish hooked onto the first cast, he'd earn less respect and yield far less satisfaction.

We hear rumors from our fishing brethren that sonar fish detection devices are now widely used in fishing. A newsletter of the Izaak Walton League reports:

> The latest thing in sonar fish detecting, now called "hydro-acoustics," is a computerized affair that not only shows you where the fish are beneath your boat but also measures them for you. Another model displays an image in perspective, or three dimensions. This $450 unit will rotate the image to show you what the bottom looks like beneath your boat when viewed from four different sides. Fish appear as small, medium or large on the display screen, and a "fish alarm" will even screen out small ones and let you know when a big fish is inside the sonar field of "view."

The community of sport fishing regards such devices with contempt. One of them says:

> I don't have a problem with fish "flashers," but the new ones that provide images of fish in color right below your boat— the (Great Lakes) boats with fax machines that get satellite information—it's just an obscene thing to me.

In the words of a special Citizens' High-Tech Review Committee set up by Wisconsin's Natural Resources Board:

> "Gadgets" are bad if their purpose is to serve as a substitute for skill and knowledge. As the skill level of the sportsperson increases, then the reliance on gadgetry should decrease.

Canoeists? If the object was simply to get from here to there by boat, you wouldn't hear people talk about white water. Once again, the idea is to challenge your skills, intelligence, coolness under pressure. Challenge is what it's all about.

Back before World War II, an earlier Waterman (Guy's father) used to take six weeks each summer to canoe the Allagash. It took a couple of days then to drive from our house in Connecticut to Maine's Moosehead Lake, and once back in the lake region there was literally no way to get back to civilization fast or even to communicate with it. When those canoes shoved off into that network of backwoods lakes above the Allagash headwaters, they were committing the half dozen occupants to their own resources for six weeks, during which they would not see more than one or two other parties. The modern Allagash runner rips down the river in a week or 10 days, elbowing other parties for the better campsites, greeting others who land on the lakes in seaplanes, never far away from communication with the outside world in the event of emergency. Could anyone suppose that the satisfaction derived from those two divergent experiences is equal?

We have a rare and precious "resource" in the backcountry, and it isn't defined by just the physical resources of trees, wildlife, streams, or even mountains. What we have to defend is the opportunity for people to get on one-to-one terms with the natural world, to experience the full challenge of the backcountry—not some phony or illusory sense fostered by well-groomed trails, bridges over every stream, and instant rescue available if you stub your toe.

Katahdin is not just Central Park 400 miles removed.

Not all the blame lies on the manager's doorstep. We hikers and backpackers tend to foster too much tameness within ourselves. Managers may simply be reading their clientele's wishes too well. The writer and backpacker Harvey Manning deplores in *Backpacker* magazine the lack of adventure in the contemporary hiking public, people who "shun a vacation on Mount Obscurity in favor of Big Deal Spire, throng Many People Camp and avoid the lonesome heart of the Godforgotten Wilderness."

The decline of adventure in the outdoors reminds us of so many forces in modern life that seek to eliminate all discomforts and difficulties. Ad writers sell electrical appliances as servants that "eliminate household drudgery." No one is supposed to wash dishes or clothes personally any more; just press a button and go watch television. We're not even supposed to brush our teeth by hand any more. Our reading habits have been steered gently away from the elegant but demanding prose style of Edward Gibbon or Sir Walter Scott to the easily digested spoon-fed *Reader's Digest* condensations.

But what remains in a life from which difficulty and work are omitted? "Too much rest itself becomes a pain," says Homer in the *Odyssey*.

All too evident today are thousands of affluent but nervous people, seeking some sort of synthetic physical challenge. In every outdoor activity that once demanded well-earned skills and genuine honest-to-God risk, you can now buy a guided weekend of imitation thrills on a guaranteed no-risk basis. Go rock climbing, scuba diving, sky diving, with some certified "expert," making sure that you only appear to be really risking danger. Your professional guide will guarantee to get you safely back to your desk on Monday morning.

Not so long ago there were corners of the globe that only the most courageous and adventurous explorers had ever seen—the arctic and antarctic snows, the remote and hidden passes and peaks of the high Himalayas, the savage wasteland of the Patagonian ice cap, to name just a few. Within the memory of living man there were literal blank spots on the map, where no one had ever been. What a treat to the imagination—what a challenge to the most resourceful of adventurers!

Today Mountain Travel and a dozen other paid professional organizations will take you to any of these places, for a fee. No experience needed. The porters will carry your tent, sahib, and cook all meals. All you do is bring lots of color film and a pair of dark glasses—and enough other fancy gear to give everyone the illusion that you're really roughing it.

Philip Levin, writing in *Appalachia* magazine, warned about this development:

> We have developed an impatience with constraints, including the constraint of unattainability. We have developed the technology to break the latter constraint, without once pausing to consider the invaluable role that the unattainable and its pursuit by visionary individuals have played in the civilization of the west.

Maybe that's a bit heavy, but the underlying thought is one we'll buy.

A few winters ago, the Appalachian Mountain Club opened two of their eight high-country huts in the wintertime, stationing a caretaker at each one. At that point, a number of winter backpackers and climbers began to fear that the AMC would ultimately open all of its high huts, thereby making it relatively easy and safe to travel in winter over high country that now affords tremendous challenge and risk to the adventurous.

Much to its credit, the AMC decided not to open up the remote winter hills in that way. The club has confined its winter facilities to the two relatively accessible huts. We applaud that decision.

In this push-button age, humanity needs recourse to difficulty. We need to encounter nature in ways that fully impress on us its enormous power and set our own efforts in perspective—feeble compared with nature's, but heroic compared with what we were tempted to shrink into.

While there is still difficulty, there is still opportunity to test what a person's made of. The hunter and fisherman know this. The birdwatcher knows it. All lovers of the outdoors tend to respond to the zest of challenge. The conservationist Bradley Snyder has written:

> It is a common observation of life that an experience that requires little yields little.... The best things, fortunately, are quite demanding.... The real benefit of the "wilderness

experience," for example, lies not in *being* in the wilderness but in taking the *initiative* in your life and getting there on your own. People do not need fresh air and sunshine half so much as they need a sense of being in command of their own minds and bodies, of planning something difficult and then doing it.

These days people want high adventure with low risk and lower personal hardship. No such thing! Joseph Wood Krutch put it most succinctly: "No cross, no crown."

We side with the sentiments expressed so well by the mountain climber Gene Prater in his book *Snowshoeing*. We commend these thoughts to the attention of all who care for maintaining the spirit of wildness in the woods and hills from New England to the Sierra and beyond:

> There is a feeling of personal insignificance standing on a high point with ridge after ridge extending to the horizon.... Man's efforts at creativity simply cannot compare with the natural scene. You may feel a deeper appreciation for the power of natural forces, not just the violence of storm and avalanche, but also the quiet Being who must have clad a thousand hills in forest, and added snow each winter to nourish the rivers and give the land a rest.
>
> We are strangers in an alien land; man doesn't belong in the winter wilderness. The mountain landscape speaks visually through its beauty and the silence of calm days of eternity, in contrast to people who are short-lived visitors. The roar of the storm does not dim the grandeur, but emphasizes that man must tread gently and with the utmost care. A gust of windblown snow and man and his snowshoe trail are gone....

Epilogue:

The Polar Bear Within

A writer only begins a book, it is the reader who completes it; for the reader takes up where the writer left off as new thoughts stir within him.

ELIZABETH YATES

WE HAVE HAD very few occasions to be in cities large enough to have zoos, but a few years ago we found ourselves in Washington, D.C., with some free hours one morning, so we went to the National Zoo. Among the exhibits, one that fascinated us was the polar bear enclosure. It included a large water tank with one glass side, so that we tourists could watch Bear swim.

We've always liked bears, and the image of the great white bear of the frozen north has especially appealed. We were enthralled watching this one magnificent beast make his passes through the tank—such power, allied to such grace and economy of effort as he soared through the water, pushed lightly off the far right corner of the tank, glided along the further side, up for air at the far left side, then swerving close to the glass, and back to the far right. With deft feather touches from his monstrous paws, he

219

guided his huge bulk effortlessly, fluently through the waters. Such magnificence in motion, such controlled wildness.

Then we looked more closely and began to notice something. Every time he crossed from one side to the other, he appeared to be traveling about the same route.

So we looked more closely still. Yes, each time when he pushed off the far right corner, the same big paw hit the same spot in the same corner. As he passed along the back of the tank, the same paw glanced off the same spot along the back of the tank. When he surfaced for air, the same two paws always pushed off the left side and guided his change of direction back along the glass front, at exactly the same level.

We began to see a time dimension to the image before us. This same white bear had been circling this same course over and over again. What else to do? The image of wildness, of power, of magnificence began to blur.

Now we looked yet more closely. We saw that where each paw landed, the paint on the concrete surface of the tank was worn off. How many times does a paw have to press against a painted surface to wear a hole in the paint?

Now the image of power and wildness was crumbling, disintegrating. We realized with horror that this glorious animal, this symbol of the spirit of wildness from the wide-open spaces of the frozen north, had been pursuing his identical passes through the little water tank—not just in a general way, but with clocklike precision and regularity—over and over and over and over again. For how many weeks or months or years? The skull that housed a bear's brain—in nature, shrewd, alert, cunning, curious, acute—now entrapped a mind destroyed by monotony. Those eyes, which could discern furtive prey on the far horizon of the ice pack and seal shadows beneath it, now registered nothing, not even us gawking tourists. The paws, which could power its journey across open arctic ocean swells or crack the skull of good-sized victims at a single swat, now lightly pressed against painted concrete eternally until the paint wore thin.

Sic transit gloria, at the National Zoo, for the diversion of the National Tourist. Sic transit wildness. Sick (*sic*).

And thus passeth much wildness on our mountainsides. We, the unthinking, unseeing hordes of hikers who mob the popular mountain trails: are we collectively repeating endlessly the same circuit? Up to the right edge of the ridge, push off with the same lug-soled paw from the top of the first summit, glance off the top of the second summit with the same paw each time, up for air (and "the view") on top of the final summit, then pushing off downhill with the same paw, and back to the valley?

Are we collectively seeing anything on this mindless repetition of the same circuit? Do we still see wildness on the mountain ridge? Do we feel the uniqueness of each day, each hour? Is every crag vivid? Do we feel ourselves a part of a magnificent mountainscape? Or do we simply wear off the paint of our tank, where we keep putting our feet in the endless recycling of our collective passing? You can see where we've worn our cage thin from passing over the treadmill the same way for years. Are we any closer to wildness than the trapped polar bear endlessly circling his caged tank in the National Zoo?

Well, of course, now we're overstating the case. As we've always seen and felt intensely, those who come to a place like the Franconia Ridge for the first time, or who return with seeing eyes and open sensibility, are finding their wilderness experience, each at his or her level, along a broad spectrum. The experience is vivid and valid for many individuals, each in his or her own way and at his or her own level. If you come to the mountains at all, you must be responding to some inward spark, some touch with the mystery of wildness. There is a bit of the polar bear in each of us, or at least it has not been stamped out of a lot of us. The problem is to give that bear a chance to roam free, unfettered, unmanaged, unmanipulated. And simultaneously to preserve, undiluted and unspoiled, the physical resource that gives us our wildness to roam in.

***

Shortly after our trip to the zoo, we saw a nature film about polar bears, which portrayed the work of scientists studying the great white predator of the arctic. One scene showed scientists drugging the bears by shooting them from an oversized snowmobile, then conducting various tests and manipulating the inert forms of the huge beasts. In fact, for most of the show, the impression left was of modern science, with its highly sophisticated toys and gadgets, its machines and powerful instruments, brooding incessantly, unrelentingly over the lives of these supposedly "wild" bears. We were left wondering whether there yet remained, in the whole wide Arctic world, any bear who went through life unharassed by a helicopter overhead, a pursuing snow machine, a drugged dart, a team of curious researchers pushing and prodding and tracking and recording and programming and probing.

Good science does not require such mischief done to the observed species. The three primatologists who have discovered so much about chimpanzees, gorillas, and orangutans (Jane Goodall, Dian Fossey, Birute Galdikas) did it all by quiet observation, not manipulative intervention. They respected their species, and were polite.

The scientists who perform this research would—perhaps will, perhaps do—deeply resent any derogation of their work. They see themselves as saving the great white bear. They are providing a solid scientific basis for understanding the polar bear's needs for habitat and food supply. With all their machines, they still brave arctic storms and a lonely, remote work station, perhaps often dull in its routines. For all we know they are underpaid and overworked. Certainly some of them love their bears and believe their work is essential to the survival of the threatened species. All true—and we apologize for bringing them into this metaphor so unfairly.

...And yet...and yet...is this truly all that is left of wildlife in the Arctic? Has our civilization reached into every corner, with its quest for arctic oil, its flying machines flitting omnisciently over the ice, its researchers observing and radio-collaring and tracking everything? Does all wildness exist only at our sufferance? Indeed, only by our deliberate intervention to save it?

Is there left any cold far waste of ice where no motor drones and no scientific progress is made, where man is not doing any beast any favors, where some great white animal pads silently its solitary way under a sky full of stars, alone?

Where the scientists go, soon follow the tour guides. Mountain Travel now arranges "historic arctic voyages aboard the icebreaker *Sovetskiy Soyuz.*" On one such voyage, a delighted participant reported:

> A bear watch from the bridge continued, and soon the helicopters took off to join the search. They reported a bear with a kill about 10 miles ahead, so the ship moved to that location. We had optimum conditions to record this exciting encounter, which brought our total of bear sightings to 22.

Read that and weep. Helicopters dispatched to locate bears for the diversion of tourists! The price of the tour, in case you're interested, is a mere $22,000 to $26,000, unless you're cheap and can tolerate roughing it in a standard $18,000 cabin on one of the lower decks rather than a suite suitable to the occasion. In the name of the arctic ice gods, will they not leave those bears alone?

When Hugh Lofting published his *Voyages of Doctor Dolittle* in 1922, the good doctor of fiction reported that he had discovered the North Pole in April 1809—by a most remarkable coincidence, precisely 100 years before Peary's second discovery of that remote site. Why did Doctor Dolittle fail to report his discovery and claim the credit that posterity has awarded to Peary? Here is the doctor's explanation, verbatim except that we substitute the word "oil" for "coal" in the original.

> Shortly after I got there the polar bears came to me in a body and told me there was a great deal of oil there.... So would I please keep it a secret.... Ah, well, it will be discovered again some day, by somebody else. But I want the polar bears to have their play-ground to themselves as long as possible. And I daresay it will be a good while yet.

Doctor Dolittle's gesture did give the bears another century and a bit more. But only a bit. Now the scientists and the oil workers and even the tourists aboard the *Sovetskiy Soyuz* follow and observe and intervene remorselessly in the lives of the once-wild bears of the frozen north.

Similarly in our own "wilderness" closer to home, we have our teams of managers droning through the woods and hills, observing and manipulating and managing the hiking "traffic," researching not just our mountain environment but us, shaping our wilderness experience to fit a management plan, pursuing us with their helicopters and their trail signs and their tent platforms and caretakers. Do we ever get to roam the forested ridge free from observation, free from weather forecasts and shuttle reservations, free from search and rescue, free from designated use patterns?

Mistake us not, we're part of the problem. No one walks the Franconia Ridge without following our cairns, treading the footway we've delineated, staying off the vegetation we're choosing to try to protect. When you turn to look for where the trail goes and you see a cairn against the sky, we put it there precisely so you would see it at that particular moment. We ourselves are part of the hovering presence of somebody else shaping your experience.

We've considered the alternatives. We've found ourselves forced to conclude that the Franconia Ridge needs this presence if the experience itself is to survive for future generations. Some friends tell us we're "manipulating" the experience of hikers walking that ridge. We wince at the word. We prefer to think of ourselves as helping our fellow hikers to see the necessity of all of us showing concern for the alpine vegetation. Education, not manipulation. Nonetheless, no matter how unobtrusively, our cairns and our dead branches and our cleared treadway are all part of the managed experience. Necessary, yes, but we pause here and now to reflect sadly on what has been lost of the wild ridge walk.

Can we hold on to whatever wildness is left? Can we preserve those opportunities for stillness and solitude, for wonder, for the freedom of the hills, for difficulty and adventure and genuine risk? This will be a test of human will and imagination. We must keep our values in focus and work hard to ward off specific influences that weaken wildness, whatever laudable objective such influences fly under. Rather we must work to strengthen those influences that maximize the vitality of the mountain world—and of ourselves, of the polar bear within.

The polar bear's status and destiny are not encouraging. So let us at least partially offset that tale by another, featuring a far more humble beast, the monarch butterfly.

One late autumn day, at our homestead in the woods of Vermont, we found a monarch butterfly with one wing badly torn. It could not fly, could only flutter a foot or so and then sink on the grass, defeated, frustrated. We admired the beauty of its one undamaged wing, spoke a kind word in a low tone, and left it on the grass. We were quite certain that before the day was out the appropriate predator would snatch up this small item on the food chain. While all other monarchs were setting sail for Texas or Mexico for the winter, this one would never make it. We had phoebes, pewees, and a great crested flycatcher around that autumn. Surely at some hour when great crested flies were in short supply, one of these flycatchers would snatch up the maimed monarch.

But the next morning, while passing the same part of our property, we noticed the one-winged butterfly again, a few feet away from its site of the day before, still fluttering, still defeated. This time we watched it a while, with pity but also with a small sense of respect for its continued struggle to survive.

On the next few mornings, we found the wounded monarch every day, but now we noticed something that chilled us to the marrow of our soul. Each morning we found that monarch about 20 to 30 feet further southwest. Wounded, maimed, defeated, doomed, that monarch still was headed for Texas, still pursued the deep ancestral impulse to do what its wild nature willed it to do. Like Martin Luther planting apple trees in a doomed world, that monarch held high its purpose in defiance of pity and pessimism, and phoebes and pewees.

On a couple of chillier mornings we held a warm hand on the frosted grass next to the monarch. He would crawl up onto the hand and rest there for as long as we would give him the time. Presumably he did so only in an instinctive reaction to warmth, but it was easy for us to read into his action something more, a bridging of the unbridgeable gulf between our species, an acceptance of our gesture of pity, concern, regret, our desire to applaud and support his unconquerable spirit.

A couple of mornings later, no monarch. Or none that we could find. Perhaps at last the great crested flycatcher took his meal. This is the way of the world.

But if we have painted too dark a picture of the prospects for wildness in some of what we said earlier, please read with us into this little parable of the maimed monarch a message of hope, or of encouragement, or of the need to hold high the spirit of wildness, and our own, in this maimed world. We do not accept the inevitable death of the spirit of wildness. It lies within the power of mankind to preserve, protect, and extend that wildness wherein lies the preservation of our world.

Like Professor Fay, we must sit up all night thinking, then walk away from the protective shelters we have built ourselves; and deliberately choose the pathless way; and "preserve the luxury of the forest to the last possible moment."

One last parable: One day we met a fellow hiker, a young woman accompanied by her boyfriend. She appeared flushed and dehydrated on a hot sunny day, and someone offered her a drink of cool water. We were going the same way, so we hiked along for a couple of miles together. A tale of pathos unfolded: this young woman's brother had been killed in a seemingly trivial tumble from a rock ledge while hiking just the previous month. This day was her first day in the mountains since that tragic event, so desolating to her family. She felt not just hot and dehydrated and sweaty and sticky, but bitterly resentful of the silent rocks and trees and the impassive mountain gods who cruelly and impersonally imposed such a fate on her only brother.

That evening we were all staying at one of the AMC's huts. It happened that this young woman fell into a long conversation with another guest who had lost close relatives to the mountain gods, but who had returned repeatedly to the mountains and arrived at some sort of accommodation with that impersonal, sometimes cruel, but ceaselessly magnificent world of rocks and trees.

The morning dawned foggy and damp. With no visibility and a cold wind, few hikers ventured above treeline. But this young woman and her boyfriend walked up into the clouds and, near the summit of the mountain, stumbled into a group of three trail maintainers at work in the silent mist. They were laboring hard to build some cairns and otherwise better define the trail through the tundra, so as to encourage hikers to stay on trail and save the alpine vegetation—to preserve the mountain environment for future generations.

The boyfriend pitched in to help move some heavy rocks. Soon the young woman joined in as well. For about an hour, up there in the silent ghostly world of mist and blowing fog, five people worked together, helping each other to help the mountain. Few words were spoken. Each had his and her private thoughts. Somewhere during that hour, wrestling stones into place, striving to protect a pathway through delicate alpine flowers, so that other young men and young women on other days might walk, gloriously alive, through the high wild mountain world—somewhere during that hour, the young woman made her peace with the mountain gods. She came to see the mountain no longer simply as brutal killer, but also as a wild world worth preserving and returning to.

We suppose that young woman returned to the valley no less grieved for her brother. But we are certain she also bore a deepened sense of the mountain world, a fuller understanding of the mystery of wildness. And we know, though our paths may never cross, that she'll be back.

In that parable lies one answer to the forces that threaten the spirit of wildness in the hills. When we commit ourselves to the mountain world, when we try to become stewards of wildness, perhaps some corner of the mystery is lifted for us, up there in the

mist and blowing fog. But only a little. In our human world interacting with that mountain world, can we find some more positive
promise than we saw standing in front of the polar bear cage at the
zoo? The wounded monarch butterfly suggests one answer. We
think that young woman showed us another answer, and it is
hopeful.

Selected Bibliography

The outpouring of concern for the wilderness environment has produced a bewildering (odd word in this context) onslaught of printed material. Sometimes it seems like too much of a good thing. The conscientious reader could spend all leisure hours reading the literature on wilderness and never set foot in the woods. We don't wish to encourage the idea that reading about it is more important than being there.

That said, however, we believe that there is a core of "must" reading, and concentric circles of valuable—informative or inspiring—thought provokers. We list below those books that we have found useful or provocative, a half dozen of which we've marked (*) as the "must" (that is, not to be allowed to become "musty") core.

Abbey, Edward. *Desert Solitaire: A Season in the Wilderness.* Simon & Schuster, 1968.

Berry, Wendell. *The Unsettling of America: Culture and Agriculture.* Sierra Club Books, 1977.

_____. *The Long-Legged House.* Harcourt, Brace & World, 1969.

Brooks, Paul. *The Pursuit of Wilderness.* Houghton Mifflin, 1971.

_____. *Roadless Areas.* Knopf, 1964.

Brower, David. *For Earth's Sake: The Life and Times of David Brower.* Peregrine Smith Books, 1990.

Callicott, J. Baird, ed. *Companion to "A Sand County Almanac."* University of Wisconsin Press, 1987.

Cohen, Michael. *The Pathless Way: John Muir and the American Wilderness.* University of Wisconsin Press, 1984.

Cole, David N. *Low-Impact Recreational Practices for Wilderness and Backcountry.* United States Forest Service General Technical Report INT-265, August 1989.

Commoner, Barry. *Making Peace with the Planet.* Pantheon Books, 1975.

Devall, Bill, and George Sessions. *Deep Ecology.* Gibbson Smith, 1985.

Dubos, René. *The Wooing of Earth.* Scribner's, 1980.

*Geisel, Theodore Seuss [Dr. Seuss]. *The Lorax.* Random House, 1971.

Grahame, Kenneth. *The Wind in the Willows,* Scribner's, 1908.

Hampton, Bruce, and David Cole. *Soft Paths.* Stackpole Books, 1988.

*Hardin, Garret. "The Tragedy of the Commons." *Science,* December 13, 1968, pp. 1243–49.

Huth, Hans. *Nature and the American: Three Centuries of Changing Attitudes.* University of Nebraska Press, 1957.

Leopold, Aldo. *The River of the Mother of God and Other Essays.* University of Wisconsin Press, 1991.

*_____. *A Sand County Almanac and Sketches Here and There.* Oxford University Press, 1949.

Levin, Philip D. Series of articles in *Appalachia:* "Toward a Recreated Wilderness: Notes on Abolishing the Four Thousand Footer Club," June 1973, pp. 132–40; "Inward to Wilderness," part 1, December 1975, pp. 49–62; part 2, December 1976, pp. 18–35; part 3, June 1978, pp. 25–44; part 4, December 1978, pp. 57–86.

Lopez, Barry, *Desert Notes: Reflections in the Eye of a Raven.* Avon Books, 1978.

Manes, Christopher. *Green Rage: Radical Environmentalism and the Unmaking of Civilization.* Little, Brown, 1990.

Marx, Leo. *The Machine in the Garden: Technology and the Pastoral Ideal in America.* Oxford University Press, 1964.

*McKibben, Bill. *The End of Nature.* Doubleday, 1989.

McPhee, John. *The Control of Nature.* Farrar, Strauss & Giroux, 1989.

_____. *Encounters with the Archdruid.* Farrar, Strauss & Giroux, 1971

*Nash, Roderick. *Wilderness and the American Mind.* Yale University Press, 1967; rev. ed., 1973, 1982.

_____. *The Rights of Nature: A History of Environmental Ethics.* University of Wisconsin Press, 1989.

Rollin, Bernard E. *Animal Rights and Human Morality.* Prometheus Books, 1981.

Runte, Alfred. *National Parks: The American Experience.* University of Nebraska Press, 1979.

Sax, Joseph L. *Mountain without Handrails: Reflections on the National Parks.* University of Michigan Press, 1980.

Schmitt, Peter. *Back to Nature: The American Myth in Urban America.* Oxford University Press, 1969; reissue, Johns Hopkins University Press, 1990.

Snyder, Gary. *The Practice of the Wild.* North Point Press, 1990.

Terrie, Philip G. *Forever Wild: Environmental Aesthetics and the Adirondack Forest Preserve.* Harbor Hill Books, 1985.

Thoreau, Henry David. *The Maine Woods.* Originally published in 1848 magazine articles and an 1864 book; see the Bramwell House edition, 1950.

*_____. *Walden; or, Life in the Woods.* 1854; see the Houghton Mifflin edition, 1893.

Waterman, Laura, and Guy Waterman. *Backwoods Ethics: Environmental Issues for Hikers and Campers,* Countryman Press, 1993.

Winner, Langdon. *The Whale and the Reactor: A Search for Limits in an Age of High Technology.* University of Chicago Press, 1989.

Index

233